HOW DO YOU LIKE IT?

Customer Services: Standardisation or Personalisation?

Victoria Schaal

This text was originally compiled as a dissertation within the University of Exeter, United Kingdom. This is an integral version of the text first published in February 2019 and updated in February 2024.

Photo on cover and design of the book by Victoria Schaal©

All rights reserved. Copyright © 2024 Victoria Schaal.

No part of this publication may be reproduced, distributed, or transmitted in any form or by any means, including photocopying, recording, or other electronic or mechanical methods, without the prior written permission of the publisher, except in the case of brief quotations embodied in critical reviews and certain other non-commercial uses permitted by copyright law.

For permission requests, write to the author, addressed:

vs@victoriaschaal.com

www.victoriaschaal.com

HOW DO YOU LIKE IT?

TABLE OF CONTENTS

Introduction	Pg. 1
Literary Review	Pg. 9
Methodology	Pg. 47
Analysis	Pg. 60
Discussion	Pg. 92
Conclusions and Limitations	Pg. 108
Bibliography	Pg. 115
Appendices	Pg. 125
About the Author	Pg. 156

A mia madre

e a Gianni

HOW DO YOU LIKE IT?

INTRODUCTION

'The customer is king' affirmed Mahatma Ghandi and today its truth is widely recognised (Kotler et al, 2009). Customers represent the fuel of businesses and are the nucleus around which the discipline of marketing revolves (Fogli, 2006; Deming, 1986; Peppers and Rogers, 2005).

However, classical marketing theory has prioritised the acquisition of new customers over their retention, a topic which has been erroneously neglected for long (Kotler et al, 2009).

Nonetheless, times have changed and both academics and companies are adapting to the novelties. Technological advancements, easily and rapidly accessible information, consumer-driven legislation and a higher level of competition in the worldwide market have led to the so called customer empowerment. Customers, in fact, have now a broader range of purchase choices and can refer to a variety of different sources of information before making their final decisions (Cook, 2010, Kotler et al, 2009; Prahald and Ramswamy, 2004). Thus, nowadays customers have become businesses' primary concern: from being predominantly product-centric, firms now tend to implement consumer-oriented strategies (Tiu Wright et al, 2006).

Retaining existing customers is just as important as acquiring new ones. It enables a business to keep competitors at arm's length, provides the grounds for long-term profitability, increases the customer base of a firm, ensuring a valuable asset, and is believed to be economical compared to seeking new customers (Kotler et al, 2009; Reinartz et al, 2005; Levitt, 1983; Fornell and Wernerfelt, 1987; Oliver, 1999).

According to several, the key to customer retention is the construction of solid long-term relationships between business and clientele. The creation of customer loyalty, the enhancement of consumer satisfaction and the increase in customer-perceived value all play a fundamental role in the generation of a robust seller-buyer bond (Gronroos, 2000; Schieffer, 2005; Kotler et al, 2009; Lovelock and Wirtz, 2004). Nevertheless, the bridge that strengthens it is the customer services department, which represents the key to the achievement of the aforementioned goals (Fogli, 2006).

Customer services are increasingly gaining more importance in entities all around the world. Over the past few decades attention to this sector from both businesses and scholars has significantly risen and studies and journal papers have spawned in academia (Schneider and White, 2004; Fogli, 2006).

The delivery of customer services is perhaps one of the most explored aspects of the topic (Schneider and White, 2004). Nonetheless, it is rather ample, multifaceted and mined by disagreements. The approach that should be undertaken by agents when interacting with customers is an area of service delivery still dominated by on-going debates. In fact, scholars present two distinct approaches that can be applied to communications: while one recommends the customisation of service according to the personal features of consumers, the other supports standardising interactions implying that every customer should be treated with the same high standards.

Although plenty has been written concerning this argument, the literature has failed to reach consensus. Generally, scholars tend to debate about the benefits and drawbacks of each approach, considering aspects like time and financial efficiency. However, their conclusions follow logical rationales based solely on theoretical material. None seems to have approached the question by also collecting primary data, such as by gathering information directly from consumers in order to understand what people favour when dealing with customer services.

The innovative aspect of this research lies in the inclusion of not solely a thorough review of theory but also direct enquiries to people in order to provide a balanced final judgment on which a conclusion can be drawn.

Researching this area not solely adds up to the existing studies about customer services and their delivery, but also contributes to the reaching of a reliable and applicable result, which scholars have not produced yet.

Several businesses nowadays invest large funds on the training of their customer services and on quality checks of their deliveries. Determining whether a best method of delivering customer services exists provides firms, especially new-born and small ones, extra knowledge on which they may base their training programs without having to seek the assistance of costly third parties.

Thus, the objectives of this study are:

a) to explore how individuals prefer customer services to be delivered and

b) to determine which approach —customisation or standardisation- is more effective at retaining customers.

HOW DO YOU LIKE IT?

LITERARY REVIEW

A customer is anyone who receives goods/services and without him, business would have no purpose (Fogli, 2006; Peppers and Rogers, 2005).

Traditional managerial literature depicts organisations as pyramids, where the management is at the top while the customers represent the bottom. However, this view has mutated and nowadays successful companies have inverted the chart, considering the customers the most important components of the organisation, thus at the top of the pyramid (Kotler et al, 2009). Many scholars too support the new perspective like Fogli (2006), Deming (1986) and Peppers and Rogers (2005), who highlight that since without clientele no business exists, the sole value a company will ever generate is the one deriving from it.

This innovative perspective transformed numerous product-centric firms into consumer-oriented organisations (Tiu Wright et al, 2006). Resultantly, the need to understand consumers' behaviours, preferences and expectations has increased and several studies aiming at establishing how to attract the greatest possible amount of customers have been carried out.

However, a vast portion of marketing theory deems

the acquisition of new customers as organisations' main goal (Kotler et al, 2009). This view is incomplete: "the purpose of a business is to find and keep customers and to get existing buyers to continue doing business with you rather than your competitors" (Levitt, 1983, Pg.101). In other words, attracting new customers is not sufficient, the business must retain them too (Reinartz et al, 2005; Levitt, 1983).

Customer retention is, thus, crucial. Firstly, as Levitt (1983) noted, it prevents buyers to seek competitors; secondly, as many estimated, acquiring new consumers can cost five times more than retaining current ones (Kotler et al, 2009; Fornell and Wernerfelt, 1987; Oliver, 1999). Moreover, customer retention contributes to customer acquisition: existing buyers are likely to spread positive information regarding the organisation in question to their social circles.

This increases the company's reputation and popularity but also represents a priceless method to attract new clients (Cook, 2010).

Yet, "the average company loses 10% of its customers each year" (Kotler et al, 2009, Pg.400), indicating that organisations' customer bases decrease regularly. Since a customer base is a market-base asset, it represents a value which a business possesses (Bell et al, 2002); hence its diminution is a loss in wealth.

Nowadays more and more companies grasp the importance of customer retention and attempt to tailor their strategies accordingly (Kotler et al, 2009). However, how to maintain a clientele in the long-term is still a pending question.

A highly significant player in consumer retention is the concept of customer-perceived value (CPV). CPV is the consumer's general assessment of the utility of a market offering based on his perceptions of what is received and what is given (Zeithaml 1988). Thus, it requires the exploration of the clientele's wants, expectations and preferences through the production of market research. This implies that understanding which are the most attractive characteristics of the offered product/service, is companies' task (Payne and Holt, 2001). Once these are identified, a CPV package is created, which includes tangibles, such as the main product, and intangibles such as the services which revolve around the product (Gronroos, 2000). Customer services fall in the latter.

Two main ingredients are required to form a CPV

package: the value proposition and the value delivery system.

"The value proposition consists of the whole cluster of product and service attributes (benefits) the company promises to deliver" (Kotler et al, 2009, Pg.388). Thus, it represents the pledge a business gives about the total experience customers will obtain from both the acquisition of the market offering and from their relationship with the entity (Kotler et al, 2009). As Cant et al. rightfully highlight, "the fulfilment of promises (...) is an important means of achieving customer satisfaction, retention of the customer base, and long-term profitability" (2009, Pg.312). However, "whether the promise is kept depends on the company's ability to manage its value delivery system" (Kotler et al, 2009, Pg.388).

"The value delivery system includes all the

experiences the customer will have on the way to obtaining and using the offering" (Kotler et al, 2009, Pg.388). An excellent one revolves around a cluster of core business processes acting as means to deliver distinctive consumer-perceived value to guarantee the customer a positive experience when interacting with the organisation (Kotler et al, 2009). Customer services represent one of these processes and play a vital role in the enhancement of the value delivery system, thus in the growth of the entire CPV package.

Several, like Dubois et al. (2007), Hooley et al. (2008) and Webster (1997), consider that effective marketing revolves around the identification, design and delivery of customer-perceived value. Supporting this view, the results of Gounaris et al. (2007)'s study suggest that delivering high CPV represents the means for a firm to generate favourable behavioural intentions.

Since it is assumed that "customers estimate which market offering will deliver the most perceived value and act on it" (Kotler et al, 2009, Pg.383), expanding CPV is crucial. In Weinstein's (2012) perspective, increasing CPV consists in simply exceeding consumers' expectations. However, Kotler et al.'s (2009) explanation is more detailed: to grow CPV a marketer may decide to either lower one of the costs the customer assumes or to enhance one or more benefits, for example customer services.

Weinstein believes that "companies that offer outstanding value turn buyers (…) into lifetime customers" (2012, Pg.4). Lovelock and Wirtz agree:

"a firm that has created social bonds with its customers has a better chance of retaining them for the long-term" (2004, Pg.370).

Nevertheless, creating solid relationships is a challenging task: "social bonds are more difficult to build than financial bonds" and "require considerable time" (Lovelock and Wirtz, 2004 Pg.370). Furthermore, once they exist, they demand constant dedication (Rust et al, 2004). This is covered by the discipline of customer relationship management (CRM), a process that explicitly recognises the long-term value deriving from existing and potential customers and which aims at increasing revenues and shareholder value through marketing activities targeting the development and enhancement of inter business-clientele relationships (Berry, 1983; Morgan and Hunt, 1994;

Gronroos, 1990).

Contrastingly, Kotler et al. (2009) provide a different definition which enlightens a new concept: the importance of information acquisition. Information gathering is a common practice in the modern world and its value often exceeds money. To obtain information, "listening to customers is crucial" (Kotler et al, 2009, Pg.402). However, people must be willing to reveal personal information. Boulding et al. (2005) believe customers are generally inclined to uncover private details to firms if they perceive it as a fair exchange of values. Nonetheless, often businesses behave opportunistically, generating mistrust in customers who become reluctant to provide information or even dishonest. With these affirmations, Boulding et al. (2005) highlight how the concept of trust is pivotal in CRM and, subsequently, in the creation of firm-customer relationships. Furthermore, they imply that it is the firm's duty to create trust in customers, contrasting Cant et al. (2009) who believe it is the actual relationship that engenders trust.

Customer services play an important role in the generation of trust. In fact, being interacting with customers their main function, agents have continuous occasions to create trust through communication, acquire valuable information about each consumer and provide the grounds on which a strong bond can start (Kotler et al, 2009).

Nonetheless, trust is not sufficient. Loyalty is "a deeply held commitment to re-buy or re-patronise a preferred product or service in the future despite situational influences and marketing efforts having the potential to cause switching behaviour" (Oliver, 1997, Pg.392). Accordingly, it is also a fundamental ingredient for relationships.

A high CPV not only cultivates long-term relationships but generates loyalty as well. However, resulting from the rise in competition in the market, acquiring customer loyalty has become harder than it used to be. Concomitantly, it has gained more importance too (Kotler et al, 2009). Schieffer (2005), for instance, believes that rendering customers loyal is at the heart of every business.

Marketing literature and companies often consider consumers as ungrateful parties, who betray brands the moment a better option is in sight. They are seen as "'brand sluts' who are most loyal to instant gratification" (Kotler et al, 2009, Pg.387).

However, contrasting views argue that the guilty parties are established brands, as they have cheated on most loyal customers by increasing costs while offering less, by chasing the fashionable segment of the moment and by limiting apologies and compensations after having committed errors. The supporters of this view, in fact, suggest that it is not loyalty to have retained many customers for long periods of time but brand inertia: a sort of laziness or reluctance to change that arises from lack of choice or from the existence of high barriers to switch seller or provider (Gounaris and Stathakopoulos, 2004).

Customer loyalty and satisfaction are often erroneously aggregated (Oliver, 1999). On the contrary, according to Stewart (1997), Oliver (1999) and Lovelock and Wirtz, the two are distinct: "the foundation for true loyalty lies in customer satisfaction" (2004, Pg.367), hence the two have a causal relationship.

Consumer satisfaction is also vital to retain buyers: research confirms that satisfied consumers have longer relationships with firms (Bolton, 1998; Zeithaml, 2000; Bowen and Ford, 2002).

Moreover, higher standards of quality result in greater levels of customer satisfaction. The quality of customer services deliveries is no exception: it strongly affects customer satisfaction as it can shape the consumer's opinion about the entity and the product/service in question (Payne et al, 1995).

Customer satisfaction also depends on the offering's overall performance in relation to the consumer's expectations. Expectations are not fixed values, they are subjective, change in time and differ pending on a broad variety of factors, including the degree of loyalty binding client and firm. Subsequently, it is utterly important to understand and manage customers' expectations. Generally, they derive from past pre and post purchase experiences, close relations' advice and marketers' and competitors' information (Kotler et al, 2009).

In contrast, they can be double bladed weapons. For instance, setting expectations too high is likely to disappoint customers, while setting them too low does not attract them (Boulding et al, 1999). To avoid this issue, attempting to understand what are customers' exact expectations is a suggestion.

Although other methods exist, direct feedback from customers may represent a valuable tool for a firm to receive a true insight of what is expected. Customer services are a means to receive and record feedback, although according to Smith (1998) their primary function is to meet the customer's expectations rather than determining them.

Nevertheless, customer services' roles "can vary widely across industries, organisations and customer segments" (Fogli, 2006, Pg.3), thus distinct definitions exist. While some are broad, where customer service is defined "as the physical distribution element of the marketing mix" (Bowen et al, 1989, Pg.78), other definitions are narrower, such as Fogli's, which suggests that a customer service represents the interaction between two parties: the customer and a member of the entity in question who "is not limited to a single function or job type within the organization" (2006, Pg.4). Shostack (1985) named such interactions service encounters (Solomon et al, 1985). These are performed through different means: live chats, emails, face-to-face meetings and phone calls. Although it has existed for a long time, "very few companies in the past had clearly defined and articulated strategies for customer service" (Payne et al, 1995, Pg.183).

Through the spread of technological automatization, the rise in competition within the market and the entities' subsequent need to gain consumers' loyalty, the role of customer services has evolved, expanded and attracted significantly more attention (Prahald and Ramswamy, 2004). In fact, in the recent decades "customer services delivery has become a catchphrase for business, as well as an inescapable part of modern life" (Fogli, 2006, Pg.XV). Resultantly, since the 1970s, both scholars and non-academics have produced studies in order to understand the various aspects of customer services (Schneider and White, 2004). Both groups tend to agree that customer services play the vital role of messengers between producer and consumer and represent the façade of an entity. Therefore, their quality greatly influences a customer's perception of a firm: when their activities are mediocre and below consumers' expectations, the whole company will be perceived by the client negatively and vice versa (Buzzell and Gale, 1987). In summary, they represent one of the most powerful means to acquire and retain customers and to create long-term relationships (Kotler et al, 2009).

From an academic perspective, customer services

are a vast topic and Schneider and White (2004) deem the delivery to be the most studied aspect. Yet, it involves a number of debates. One of them concerns the approach agents should use during service encounters in order to gather customers' personal information, exceed their expectations, construct a solid rapport and ultimately facilitate consumer retention.

The argument brought by academics revolves around two opposite approaches: the standardisation of interactions, where each client is treated in the same manner, and the customisation or personalisation of deliveries according to the individual consumers.

The focus of standardisation is mainly internal, on operations' efficiency, and its result is the provision to the customer of a homogenous experience (Porter, 1980). More specifically, standardisation relies on a set of basic pre-established criteria designed to address predicted scenarios of customer's issues and queries. This echoes Ritzer (2014)'s phenomenon of McDonalidisation, the four dimensions of which result in a form of standardisation on a global scale.

Gudergan and Hoeck explain that a "standard is in the broadest sense the result of unification (...) of products, processes, interfaces, etc (...) which has taken place within a system (e.g. company (...))" (2002, Pg.18). This iteration is substantiated by Blum et al. (2001) and Verman (1973), although they apply it more specifically to organisational processes rather than customer services.

Mörschel et al., however, express a different perspective: "a standard (…) is the result of a simplification" (2007, Pg.259). Simplifying is a synonym of disentangling, breaking down; hence it is the antonym of unifying. The truth is that standardisation is based on both and Gudergan and Hoeck (2002) recognise it, 'though not explicitly. In fact, they write that standardised results are achieved through the formation of specific and separate qualification measures, which establish how a service must be provided. The quality of such results is further supported by uniform processes for the evaluation of the offered service (Gudergan and Hoeck, 2002). Therefore, standardisation first involves simplifying and disassembling a service delivery and then unifying the outcomes to facilitate its assessment.

Examples of pre-established measures are omnipresent in service encounters: from the set corporate greetings and closings (thanking, using the brand name, offering extra help) to the calculated, predictable language used by agents (set phrases, enthusiastic expressions). All these predetermined criteria have one goal: to provide the same, replicable, homogenous, positive experience to every customer.

Great benefits arise from standardisation. Standardising the procedures of a customer service through the use of specific criteria and norms defines the exact way it has to be delivered. This minimises potential errors (Gudergan and Hoeck, 2002) and reduces the duration of service encounters, diminishing time wastes, a benefit for both busy and hasty consumers and firms targeting efficiency (Lovelock et al, 2014).

A uniform format benefits companies as it diminishes transaction costs too (Gudergan and Hoeck, 2002). For instance, training the personnel is cheaper as the same formation can be given to multiple agents and at the same time if needed. It is also simpler for trainees to learn as the establishment of criteria provides specific guidelines to follow. This also endows businesses with more freedom to hire/fire: set personnel qualifications facilitate the recruitment of suitable employees (Gudergan and Hoeck, 2002).

Comparison is also enhanced by standardisation (Woods et al, 1986; Gudergan and Hoeck, 2002). For customers, standardised services represent clearly structured offers which provide them with a clearer price-performance comparison, simplifying the distinction of entities that offer poor service from those that deliver an excellent one (Mörschel, 2002). For organisations, easy comparison encourages a fair and objective competition among the agents.

Ultimately, standardisation engenders equality. Since processes, approaches and requirements are specifically outlined, they are usable with an enormous variety of people. This compatibility reduces discrimination and bias as everyone is given the same treatment regardless of their individual characteristics (Schuh, 2000),

"Some managers believe that services cannot be standardised -that customisation is essential for providing high-quality service" (Lovelock et al, 2014, Pg.311). However, Lovelock et al (2014) contrast this view explaining that, in the context of non-professional services such as retailing, it is possible to standardise services indeed, as these often involve tasks of a routine nature.

Nonetheless, if on one hand standardisation involves some valuable benefits, it also presents some heavy limitations. The approach, for instance, through homogenisation, creates an easily forgettable experience (Ritzer, 2014), as nothing in the service encounter is unique. It also causes a poor or null engagement of the customer and can be perceived by some individuals as a dull, tedious and boring event.

The greatest drawback of standardisation, however, is that it does not consider the unexpected. Agents are formed to deal with a certain number of scenarios and to follow a script. The moment a situation differs from the predicted ones, the agents find themselves unprepared and the results are disappointing. As Payne et al. outline, "customers and their behaviour cannot be standardized and totally predetermined" (1995, Pg.87). Service encounters are not simplistic events. They involve various kinds of situations, each implying different sets of circumstances overwhelmed by distinct moods, tones and conducts. It is impossible for a firm to anticipate them all; hence standard procedures for each case cannot be established. By the same token, agents cannot predict all consumers' requests or complaints. However, they could be trained to adopt their creativity and use an innovative behaviour in order to adapt to each customer's situation. This is the foundation of customisation.

Customisation emphasises an external focus on the

customer, implying that the entity needs to be flexible in order to provide the consumer with a unique experience (Porter, 1980).

Practical examples of customisation are: going the extra mile (offering a bonus, a discount or making an exception), building rapport through asking personal questions, using the information mentioned by the customer in order to create an engaging conversation instead of a dry interrogation. The final objective of such a practice is to create a unique, personalised and inimitable conversation.

Several academics substantiate the approach. Kotler et al., for instance, suggest that customer services should "communicate in a personalised way" with the clientele and "customise products, services and messages to each customer" in order to acquire more personal information and to build strong firm-client bonds (2009, Pg.398).

Other supporters are Pine and Gilmore who even define customer services as "intangible activities customized to the individual request of known clients" (1999, p. 8). Their fame, however, derives from what they called experience economy, which refers to our current situation as an advanced service economy that has started to market a mass customisation of service offerings (1999). Resultantly, they suggest that a business should perform in a way that is hoped to please the clientele. The target is delivering a positive experience that can be remembered, talked about and used as a basis for future purchase decisions. The ultimate goal is the enhancement of the CPV of the company's offerings and the production of repeat business. This rationale turns the remembrance of the experience into the actual market offering (Pine and Gilmore, 1999).

Experience economy echoes the concept of experiential marketing. Coined by Schmitt (2000), it is based on the assumption that consumers do not simply buy but also want to be stimulated, entertained and challenged by the goods/services they purchase. Hence, experiential marketing's main goal is to create and deliver positive, comprehensive experiences to customers (Schmitt, 2000).

Both concepts revolve around customisation and the idea that the act of purchasing is only a small part of the long-term experience of being a customer. However, only Pine and Gilmore (1999) explicitly state that personalisation is the key to growing CPV. In fact, they explain that customising a product turns it into a service, while customising a service transforms it into an experience and customising an experience produces a transformation in customer-perceived value (1999).

Nevertheless, Kotler et al. (2009) deem Pine and Gilmore (1999)'s work incomplete. Firstly, they argue that "not all purchasing 'experiences' need such a pronounced emphasis on the experiential attributes of a CPV offering" and make the example of commodities (Kotler, 2009, Pg.411). Deriving from this observation, they draw that "the experience economy is a relationship marketing concept that needs to be interpreted by providers, in an appropriate way for their market activities" (Kotler, 2009, Pg.411).

Secondly, the concept of experience economy recommends personalisation (Pine and Gilmore, 1999). However, personalising the communication risks to be perceived by some as over friendly, thus unpleasant and irritating (Kotler, 2009). Nevertheless, given that it is highly subjective, only people's opinions can confirm this point.

Ultimately, they underline that identifying the components of a business experience is key (Kotler et al, 2009). What is the ideal experience an organisation needs to offer in order to retain customers? How should customer services agents be trained in order to provide it? These are questions which Kotler et al. (2009) accuse Pine and Gilmore (1999) of not having addressed and they attempt to provide the answers. In their view the customer does not solely receive the experience created by the business, but contributes to its formation: it is a matter of co-creation arising from high quality and personalised interactions which enable individual consumers to co-generate unique experiences. However, the attractiveness of an experience is determined by the presentation and competences a company provides when producing the final market offering (Kotler et al, 2009). Smith (1998) contests this point: since expectations are defined by the customer himself, the attractiveness of an experience is subjective and depends on potential consumers' preferences.

Kotler et al. (2009) recommend a training program based on listening and using the heard information to build a positive experience. Deighton (1996) provides a similar advice through his interactive marketing. Although it relates more specifically to the Web, the term depicts the capacity of addressing consumers, remembering what they said and serving them in a way that demonstrates that their words are remembered (Deighton, 1996).

Lovelock and Wirtz add that "customers tend to value the extra attention given to their needs (…) including efforts to meet special requests", thus training should revolve around the appropriate and timely provision of preferential treatment (2004, Pg.370).

Nevertheless, no approach is flawless and customisation is no exception. For instance, it is particularly difficult to achieve: it requires the acquisition of information which, being time-consuming, involves higher costs. There is also a risk of the agents 'letting themselves go', leading to a higher level of forgetfulness and a lower degree of professionalism, impacting both the customer experience and the achievement of a suitable solution to the query. Moreover, although the approach may be very appreciated by some individuals, others may perceive it as false-friendly, disrespectful, invasive or even unprofessional. The gathering of private information can be especially tricky: too many personal questions may resemble an interrogation which is generally regarded as irritating or, by some, as a violation of privacy.

Ultimately, as noted by Smith (1998), building rapport requires time. Lengthy encounters undermine the efficiency of customer services, affecting the finances of a business, and potentially irritate customers who might be in a rush or who may simply prefer to go straight to the point.

Sometimes the line separating customisation and standardisation is fine. On some occasions, what apparently is a way to personalise the interaction is actually one of the several calculated, standard measures. An example is the use of the customer's name. Asking for and using it may be considered as a form of customisation. However, it is actually commonplace, especially in Anglophone cultures, and a strongly encouraged practice during training programs. Thus, in reality, it is a pre-set and calculated criterion meant to be applied to all customers and the result is a homogeneously customised communication which does not aim to be unique.

In contrast, customised communications often present a few elements of standardisation too (Lovelock et al., 2014). A set corporate opening and closing, for instance, is indeed a form of standardisation, which the interaction benefits from as it conveys seriousness and professionalism.

Nevertheless, these examples do not refer to components of the core conversation between agents and clients, but represent solely the ornaments of the interaction. Hence, their impact on the encounter's level of customisation/standardisation is minor. The result is not a combination of approaches: a conversation may still be totally personalised even 'though it contains elements of standardisation and vice versa.

While all the aforementioned scholars have highlighted the differences between the two approaches, including benefits and drawbacks of each, none has asked directly to individuals how they prefer to be treated when dealing with customer services. Academics have conjectured about consumers, they attempted to estimate how some individuals may react to certain approaches and made assumptions. Yet, none has verified such thoughts. The next chapter of this dissertation focuses on the collection of primary data in order to gather real information and put a full stop to the numerous conjectures in this field.

HOW DO YOU LIKE IT?

METHODOLOGY

"A methodology is an approach to the process of the research" (Collis and Hussey, 2009, Pg.73). Morgan and Smirchich (1980) separated the various methodology paradigms on a continuum, the two opposite extremes of which are positivism and interpretivism.

A research's methodology is selected on the basis of the phenomenon/issue under study (Creswell, 2003). In this case interpretivism is the most suitable choice, as it is an inductive methodology, which focuses on gathering rich qualitative data and "on exploring the complexity of social phenomena with a view to gaining interpretive understanding" (Collis and Hussey, 2009, Pg.57).

Contrasting positivism, interpretevism lies on the assumption that social reality is highly subjective, as it is influenced and tailored by individuals' perceptions: "the world is in part what one makes of it" (Morgan and Smircich, 1980, Pg.494). More specifically, the paradigm considers that, since every individual has their own perception of reality, then several realities exist. Hence, interpretivism seeks to explore these subjective multiple realities, implying that a certain degree of bias always exists (Creswell, 1994; Collis and Hussey, 2009).

This assumption represents a fundamental difference between positivism and interpretivism and is the main reason why the latter is deemed to be more appropriate for this research: the area under study is indeed a complex social phenomenon and the questions that this dissertation attempts to answer are completely based on individuals' opinions, preferences, expectations and perceptions.

Moreover, qualitative data is deemed to generate a higher level of validity as it is richer in detail and considers the existence of various nuances within a problem (Coolican, 1992). When it comes to discovering humans' thoughts, it is hardly a simplistic black-and-white matter.

Qualitative data, however, guarantees a lower level of reliability (Collis and Hussey, 2009): if this research was replicated, the results would likely differ as not all individuals share the same perspective and these can mutate in time. Nonetheless, this research aims at understanding people's opinions and their reasons. Thus, the concept of validity and replicability are irrelevant as this dissertation does not attempt to establish a rule or calculate frequency or find a solution to a specific problem.

A method is a technique for gathering/analysing primary data (Collis and Hussey, 2009). The methods belonging within this paradigm "seek to describe, translate and otherwise come to terms with the meaning, not frequency of certain more or less naturally occurring phenomena in the social world" (Van Maanen, 1983, Pg.9). Given that the aim of this dissertation is to explore customers' perspectives in relation to service encounters, the chosen data collection method for this research is semi-structured in-depth interviews.

Since interviews' purpose is to explore and gather "data on understandings, opinions, what people remember doing, attitudes, feelings and the like" (Arksey and Knight, 1999, Pg.2), they are an adequate method to discover this research's targeted findings.

As suggested by Easterby-Smith et al. (1991), semi-structured interviews are favoured over unstructured ones when it is important to comprehend the construct on which the interviewee grounds his/her opinions about a specific situation. In this case, it is pivotal to discover the reasons why the participants prefer customised or personalised customer services deliveries so that training programs can consider these motives and adapt to them. Thus, the interviews include a number of pre-prepared open ended questions combined with probes improvised during the meetings on the basis of the participants' responses (see App.1 for prepared questions list).

The fact that the majority of questions have been pre-established is to avoid the need of major clarifications, which may influence the participant's response, leave room for misinterpretations and waste time. Open ended questions have been favoured as they allow individuals to freely express their own perceptions and opinions without restrictions, enabling the gathering of richer data in terms of details.

It is, however, important to note that open questions reduce comparability of results and consistency (Collis and Hussey, 2009). Nevertheless, as asserted previously, the main target of this data gathering is not to discern a pattern or some analytical explanation, but to explore an exclusively social phenomenon. Thus a lower degree of comparability does not represent a major drawback in this case.

The interviews are conducted face-to-face to provide the interviewer with the opportunity to gather further information and/or expand on areas mentioned by the participants, which might trigger interest for the research's purpose. Having a visual contact with the interviewee also provides an insight of how confident and sure he/she is of his/her response, an important factor which helps assessing whether the participant is truly affirming his/her own perspective.

Additionally, this type of encounters eliminates no responses and prevents the occurrence of questionnaire fatigue, defined as the feeling of reluctance arising in people to fill out unsolicited forms (Wallace and Mellors, 1998).

Although the interviews are recorded and then transcribed, the participants' identities remain anonymous. Concerning sample choices, since the focus of the interpretivist approach is on the quality of the data rather than the quantity, the sample is small (Collis and Hussey, 2009). Yet, it allows a deeper analysis of the data gathered and reduces the risk of overlooking important details. Moreover, the sample is not random: 10 people have been selected based on age and gender in order to provide a wider variety of individuals to interview. The list of participants is displayed in table 1.

Table 1

Female	Age Group	Age	Nationality	Profession
F1	18-29	20	French	University student
F2	30-39	30	Italian	Marketing researcher
F3	40-49	43	British	Nurse
F4	50-59	50	Italian	Writer and journalist
F5	>60	62	British	Painter
Male				
M1	18-29	25	Singapore	University student
M2	30-39	34	British	IT specialist
M3	40-49	47	German	Photographer
M4	50-59	55	American	Waiter
M5	>60	70	French	Manager

Furthermore, a varied sample diminishes the limitation deriving from its size and enhances the study's generalisability, which is "the extent to which you can come to conclusions about one thing (often a population) based on information about another (often a sample)" (Vogt, 1993, Pg.99). Gummesson (1991) and Normann (1970) explain that in interpretivist studies it is perfectly possible to generalise form a limited range of cases, even a single one, provided that the prior analysis has accurately captured interactions and features of the phenomenon under study (see App.2 for examples of interviews).

Qualitative data collection presents a few challenges. The main one is due to the fact that there is "no clear and accepted set of conventions for analysis corresponding to those observed with quantitative data" (Robson, 1993, Pg.370). However, qualitative approaches have been elaborated and are incredibly diverse, complex and nuanced (Holloway and Todres, 2003). The data collected in this research will be analysed through a combination of two approaches: the thematic analysis and the general analytical procedure.

A thematic analysis enables the discovery of themes and concepts embedded in transcriptions (Rubin and Rubin, 1995). "A theme captures something important about the data in relation to the research question and represents some level of patterned response or meaning within the data set" (Braun and Clarke, 2006, Pg.10). By unearthing and analysing themes, the method not solely describes the collected data, but also interprets various aspects of the research topic (Boyatzis, 1998). Therefore, thematic analysis is deemed to reflect reality by scraping off its surface to penetrate deeper. Being very flexible, it is an indispensable research tool, which can uncover a rich and detailed, yet complex account of data (Braun and Clarke, 2006).

Being untied to any paradigm, the general analytical procedure is a method by which large volumes of qualitative data can be managed and analysed (Miles and Huberman, 1994). The first step is to identify codes within the data, categorising them in terms of priority and extrapolating the main ones to form themes (see App.3 for example of coded transcript). The researcher plays an active role in highlighting themes (Taylor and Ussher, 2001), thus the selection requires careful reflections (see App.4 for map of themes). Summaries at this stage may be required in order to construct solid generalisations representing the grounds of a new theory.

HOW DO YOU LIKE IT?

ANALYSIS

Analysing the interviews disclosed interesting preliminary observations.

Firstly, all interviewees confirm relying on customer services regularly and the numerous examples they provided demonstrates it. The main reason is the encountering of issues, thus post-purchase situations, as 9 out of 10 affirm. Only 4 mention pre-purchase occasions, like information requests.

Secondly, all reveal having had varied customer service experiences in terms of quality. They all depict negative and positive ones. However, when questioned about positive remembrances, a few individuals showed some hesitation before starting to tell their story, as if they needed a few seconds to recall an example. Interestingly, no one showed any difficulty in remembering a negative experience.

Nevertheless, the combination of the general analytical procedure and the thematic analysis has permitted the unearthing of significant themes.

HOW DO YOU LIKE IT?

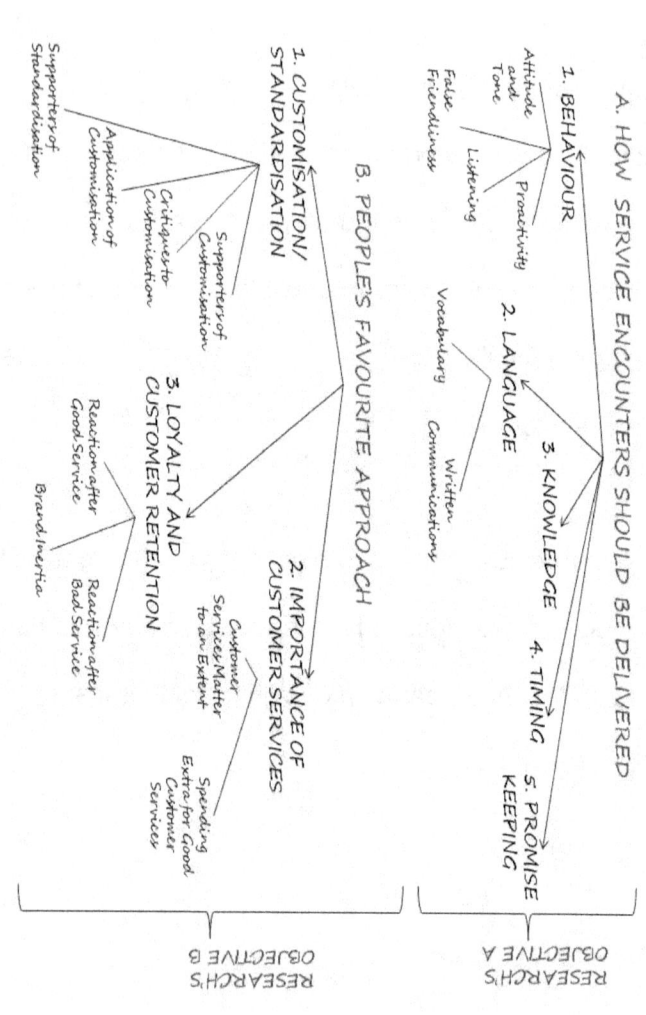

Part A

The research's objective 'a' is to explore how people prefer customer services to be delivered. From the interviewees' responses, it emerges that individuals have a clear and precise idea of how they would like to be served by customer services. Through the descriptions of their experiences, they illustrate exactly what they prefer, despise and expect from agents.

1. Behaviour

1.1 Attitude and Tone

Agents' attitude and tone appear to weigh greatly on the interviewees' judgments. Politeness and kindness, for example, are highly regarded. In fact, when depicting their experiences, they all severely criticise agents who were impolite, while they praise friendly and kind ones.

Moreover, the participants appear to be very sensitive to rudeness, which is described in detail by all participants. F4, for example, affirms that:

"the lack of kindness is unacceptable for me. It happened to me…to see agents being…rude…and impolite. They interrupted me….they used…monosyllabic answers…and their attitude was absolutely negative and arrogant ".

This feeling is commonplace among the interviewees, who unanimously condemn such behaviours and consider politeness and friendliness indispensable.

F3, M2 and M5, however, also mention the importance of facial expressions and encourage smiling pending on circumstances:

"[an agent] must have an attitude according to the situation. If it is a small problem (...) he must be smiley. If it is a very difficult problem, (...) he must not smile" (M5).

The two oldest female participants, F5 and F4, highlight that agents should also show respect, particularly with the elderly:

"it's very important...err...to speak not too quickly. Err...sometimes I see very old people having a lot of problems with...err...customer services because...err...agents on the other side don't care about who they're talking to and if the customers are writing down what they say" (F4).

1.2 False Friendliness

If on one hand interviewees insist on the use of politeness, they also condemn false friendliness, which emerges from the responses of half the participants. All explicitly express their dislike as it does not sound natural.

F1 also explains that there must be coherence between the two to avoid sounding false friendly:

"it's not all about the words you use. It's also about body language".

1.3 Proactivity

The concept of proactivity and helpfulness emerge from the responses of 7 interviewees out of 10. In particular, the participants mention episodes in which agents refused to help resolve their query. F3, for instance, criticises the agent as:

"[the agent] she was always saying that she could not do this, could not help and stuff...(...) the lady clearly didn't want to work".

Similar words are pronounced by other participants too, like F5 and M4, whose bad experiences also revolved around the agent's reluctance to help. From these reflections, it emerges that customers expect agents to show a proactive behaviour.

1.4 Listening

From the perspective of 6 participants:

"the most important thing agents should focus on is listening" (F3).

This opinion derives from the numerous occasions the interviewees describe in which agents did not listen to them and misunderstood their queries. Listening, showing interest and paying close attention to the customer's words are, thus, crucial as well as being more effective. In fact, misunderstandings not solely irritate customers, but waste time, as a few participants noted. As a solution to this issue, M5 advises agents to summarise the customer's query in order to make sure they understood correctly.

2. Language

2.1 Vocabulary

2.1.1 Negations

In terms of vocabulary, the participants made precise suggestions. F3, for instance, depicts occasions in which agents used a vocabulary she did not appreciate:

"[the agent] was only using negations...'I cannot', 'I'm not able', 'I can't help' (...) agents should avoid rudeness both in terms of vocabulary and of attitude" (F3).

2.1.2 Positive Words

Instead, the participants encourage the

use of a kind vocabulary and what some of them call positive words:

"words like 'have a great day' or 'I hope you'll be pleased with your purchase'" (F3).

2.1.3 Jargon

Many interviewees complain about employees' frequent use of jargon. All reprehend it but, as highlighted by F1, the explanations must not be over-simplistic either:

"[agents] should really work on (...) using vocabulary that's accessible to everyone (...) don't use jargon, but don't baby-talk me either".

2.2 Written Communications

2.2.1 Format

In written customer services, interviewees agree that formalities are to be respected where tidiness is combined with polite and adequate greetings, sign-offs and closing pleasantries:

"agents just need to write correctly following the format of a business letter. They should write neatly, (…) explain carefully the solution" (M4).

2.2.2 Grammar Errors

Mistakes in written customer services communications appear to be common given that all participants mention having spotted them on numerous occasions.

Everyone criticises agents' committing errors, as nowadays, internet and checkers allow their avoidance very easily.

Yet, the interviewees do not seem to react in the same way. Some judge written errors severely, considering them unacceptable as they do not convey professionalism and give the impression the agent is not dedicated enough.

Others are more lenient: although they regard errors as irritating and believe they are best to be avoided, they also assert that if they are minor or do not greatly affect the sense of the text, they generally overlook them:

"errors are not to be made. They're not professional at all. And also, agents are paid to do the job, so they should do it well. Nonetheless, if the mistakes are minor and the email contains the right information I need, then I don't care anymore" (M5).

3. Knowledge

Agents' lack of knowledge and poor preparation concerning the organisation they work for and its products is reprehended by a few when describing their negative experiences:

"half of the time they don't really know how to solve my problems" (M1).

What surfaces from these criticisms is that

individuals discern immediately whether an employee is unsure or incompetent and that they expect agents to be fully knowledgeable in relation to their employer and their tasks.

4. Timing

Timing is a theme which emerges in several responses and in numerous occasions. Interviewees consider that timing and efficiency are pivotal as people are busy and have no time to waste. They compliment agents who provide a rapid service, while they diminish those who take a long time to solve the query. The general consensus is that:

"agents should learn how to be quick but very often they take ages" (F3).

5. Promise keeping

Agents not keeping their promises are the protagonists of many participants' negative experiences. Interviewees insist on the fact that keeping promises is crucial:

"if a customer service agent says that they're going to do something for you (...)they should fulfil a quotation of what they said that they're gonna do" (M2).

Part B

The research's objective 'b' is to determine which approach among customisation and standardisation is more effective at retaining customers. Each interviewee appears to generally favour one specific approach over the other but to an extent.

6. Customisation vs Standardisation

6.1 Supporters of Customisation

Generally, although the divide is not drastic, customisation is substantiated by more interviewees than standardisation (6 against 4). Supporters provide examples of customer services deliveries that had been personalised to their features and explain why the treatment was appreciated. Generally, they affirm that customised encounters make them feel unique, special and taken care of:

"I like when they personalise the conversation. It makes me feel…unique" (F3).

F1 adds that they convey a more human and natural atmosphere. M5, however, also highlights that customisation is necessary, as he believes his issues are not necessarily the ones other customers encounter.

6.1.1 Customisation Retains Customers

A few participants state that the personalisation of services led them to become loyal to an entity. F5, for instance, remembers the first time she went to her favourite tea house and how the waitress provided her with tasters so she could select her favourite. The waitress also understood that F5 was in the mood for a chat and stopped to talk accordingly. This personalised approach, as F5 asserts, pleased her and rendered her a regular customer:

"She understood that we loved different

kinds of teas and she brought us a selection. She also understood we liked chatting and she stopped to talk with us. She was absolutely divine. I loved the way I was treated and now I go to that tea house only".

6.1.2 How to Customise

Among the supporters of customisation, F2 not solely praises the approach but also provides a suggestion for agents to personalise their delivery. In fact, in her view:

"They [agents] need to identify the customer's needs to provide the best service possible. So, we need to find out what the customer wants…hmm… what the customer is after and then based on that, provide the service or products that are required. They also need to (…) try to discover and find out information from the customer. (…) Building a rapport is essential" (F2).

6.2 Critiques to Customisation

6.2.1 Time

The supporters of customisation present one important objection to the approach: the availability of time. For example, F2 explains that:

"if I'm in a rush and stuff, I don't appreciate that. If I have some spare time and I'm in a fairly good mood then that is fine".

Time waste is one of the two main points standardisation supporters criticise customisation for. M4's words, for instance, explain this very synthetically:

"agents waste a lot of time with irrelevant blathering and useless chats which only make me waste my time and patience".

6.2.2 Personal Information

Nevertheless, the most significant point that drives some participants to oppose customisation is the sharing of personal information. M4 admits:

"I really don't like when they (…) try to use your personal information to please you more. My life is my life and I don't want to share it with strangers".

These words are echoed by M1, who adds that asking private details is disrespectful.

6.3 Application of Customisation

Given that customisation is both praised and criticised pending on subjective factors, like spare time and mood, understanding when the approach can be applied is vital:

"tailoring the conversation can be a good thing, but I think the customer service agent needs to be fully aware of when he can actually apply that tailored approach" (M2).

Nonetheless, it can be challenging for agents to establish whether the service encounter requires a personalised approach. F4 attempts to provide a solution:

"I think you must watch and listen to…err…to the people and the way people explain themselves. You can exactly…err…imagine what kind of person you have beside you. And… in that way you can personalise your service."

6.4 Supporters of Standardisation

Not many describe an experience of standardised customer service. A potential reason, as M4 illustrates, is that customised communications are average and do stand out in everyday life; therefore, they are easily forgettable.

Nonetheless, standardisation supporters substantiate the approach for the fairness it seems to engender and the bias it minimises:

"agents should avoid bias as much as possible and treat everyone the same. Of course, they must treat each person well, with high standards" (M4).

Another reason for favouring standardisation is its promptness and velocity:

"a good service should always follow a standard procedure based on effectiveness and rapidity" (M3).

7. <u>Importance of Customer Services</u>

Generally, the importance of customer services is a point of consensus between the interviewees. With the exception of one participant, M1, they agree on the fact that customer services are a significant part of entities. Accordingly, they also reveal that their performance affects to a great degree both their opinion on the organisation and their purchase behaviour:

"customer services are the façade of a business, thus it's obvious that they will affect my opinion" (F3).

7.1 Customer Services Matter to an Extent

Customer services are the not the sole factor to influence customers' behaviour, as some participants iterate. For example, M3 states:

"it's not only the customer services that encourage me to purchase. There are also other factors like the price, the quality, my finances and needs...and more."

7.2 Spending Extra for Good Customer Services

Several participants reveal their willingness to pay more for a better customer service as they believe that an efficient post-purchase service might be needed in the future and save precious time:

"the extra money is almost always worth the safety. I don't like problems, you see? I'm a busy man, I have no time to waste. If I need something, I want it fast and working. If this involves more money, I'll pay cause it will save me time which to me is money" (M3).

Nevertheless, some pontificate that the extra spending is worth especially when high involvement purchases are made:

"being able to trust in post-purchase support will make me willing to pay more, particularly on larger purchases" (M4).

8. Loyalty and Customer Retention

8.1 Reaction after Good Service

From several responses, it emerges that good customer services' quality not solely influences consumers' purchase behaviour, but also that it engenders loyalty and facilitates consumer retention:

"I write down the companies that I like according to some criteria. Customer services are one of these criteria and if I'm pleased I will buy from them again" (M3).

This is reflected also in F3's words. In fact, she asserts that the excellent service Amazon agents provided her encourage her to purchase more from the entity. F4 shares the same feeling.

8.2 Reaction after Bad Service

Although they shared similar reactions after good customer services, the participants express contrasting opinions concerning poor encounters. The majority judges' strictly and shares M5's perspective:

"a bad service for me it's a very bad image and I will try in the future not to buy from them".

Some, like M3, admitted noting on a black list the companies whose customer services dissatisfied them.

The minority, however, is more lenient and tends to give one more chance after a negative experience:

"you can't brand a company as being the good nor bad through one communication" (M2).

M3, however, expresses his willingness to

give an additional possibility provided that the business offers him a form of compensation for the poor service.

8.3 Brand Inertia Exists

Nevertheless, avoiding an organisation because of its poor service is not always possible. This phenomenon is called brand inertia and is abhorred by the participants. In fact, half of the interviewees mention occasions in which they wished to change provider but were unable due to a lack of choice or high barriers to stop the business connection:

"sometimes it's just not possible to avoid companies that provide a bad service. For example, I hate my bank and their customer services are useless. Still, changing would be a big hassle which honestly I'm not prepared to face. I'm lazy and that makes me loyal" (F3).

HOW DO YOU LIKE IT?

DISCUSSION

When Fogli defined customer services as "an inescapable part of modern life" (2006, Pg.XV), he was correct: the numerous experiences the interviewees describe confirm it.

Schneider and White (2004) write that customer services' importance is expanding and the participants' thoughts echo their opinion indeed. F4, for instance, defines customer services as:

"the business card of a company".

Furthermore, several participants confirm their

willingness to pay a higher price for a better customer service.

These findings undoubtedly support what scholars believe: nowadays customer services play a crucial role; subsequently it is primordial for businesses to focus concrete attention and funds on their adequate formation.

Nevertheless, this research digs deeper. In fact, it attempts to establish on what exactly organisations need to form their agents.

In relations to objective 'a', the data reveals that customers have clear expectations on how agents should serve and precise criteria on which they evaluate customer services that are untied to any approach.

Concerning employees' conduct, the participants all agree that a good agent should display a helpful and proactive behaviour and his attitude must be kind, polite and friendly at all times. An ancient Chinese proverb says 'a man without a smiling face must not open a shop'. According to the participants, there is truth in these words as they consider smiling very important, pending on circumstances.

Furthermore, the fact that interviewees remembered agents' rudeness vividly underlines that such a conduct is unacceptable.

However, Kotler et al. (2009), mention the potential risk of conveying false friendliness. Their opinion reflects the participants' responses, which explicitly discourage the abuse of kindness and unanimously condemn false friendliness.

The interviewees' numerous descriptions of negative experiences, in which agents ignored or misunderstood their queries, indicates that listening closely to consumers is crucial. This observation supports Kotler et al. (2009)'s and Deighton (1996)'s affirmations.

In terms of language, the use of negations and phrases that convey a lack of helpfulness or knowledge irritate the participants and are to be avoided. Instead, positive words and a generally energetic and enthusiastic vocabulary should be used. Agents should also pay particular attention to jargon. As the participants iterate, some terms might be commonplace for individuals operating in specific sectors, but may mean nothing to others.

Concerning written communications, business

format texts appear to suffice to please consumers. However, although some interviewees affirm that in specific circumstances they may overlook them, they unanimously agree that errors are not to be committed. Regardless of their importance and nature, mistakes do not convey a sense of dedication and show poor professionalism and competence.

Moreover, agents' lack of knowledge about their employers and their goods/services is deemed unacceptable. Consumers expect agents to be fully prepared and their responses indicate that they easily discern whether an employee is unsure or incompetent. Accordingly, organisations must ensure that all the relevant information is taught to the labour adequately.

Furthermore, several participants highlight how unfulfilled promises undermine the image they have of the organisation in question and their loyalty. They encourage making promises only when they can be kept; otherwise, it is best to avoid making them. Their thought confirms Cant et al. (2009)'s belief that promise keeping is fundamental to satisfy and subsequently retain the clientele.

Although these observations may seem obvious, thousands of deliveries from small and large companies' customer services still do not meet such basic standards, as the interviewees' personal experiences amply demonstrate. This underlines the urgency for businesses to amend and improve their customer services training and pay particular attention to the aforementioned themes emerging from the analysis and highlighted by academics.

Organisations need to provide services which meet/exceed customers' expectations if they want to retain customers. In fact, the data reveals that the majority of the participants try to avoid as much as possible companies that served them poorly. Only a few is willing to give the entity an extra chance.

It is, however, true that the participants also mention situations of brand inertia, in which they have no choice but to remain loyal to entities, although these have provided mediocre services, just like Gounaris and Stathakopoulos (2004) explained. Yet, companies must not rely on it as a source of customer retention: brand inertia has time limits (i.e. contracts end) and it contributes to the spreading of negative publicity arising from the frustration of trapped customers.

With regards to objective 'b', as explained in the Literature Review chapter, scholars have written extensively about standardisation and customisation but distinctively. None has envisaged the possibility of customers not always preferring the same approach. The primary data, however, reveals that it is precisely the case: customers do not always favour one approach over the other. Their preferences change pending on their availability of time and their mood.

According to the data, the main drawbacks of customisation are the considerable amount of time it requires and its use of customers' personal information, as Smith (1998) and Boulding et al. (2005) respectively predicted.

Concomitantly, the rapidity and efficiency of agents to resolve queries is the primary benefit of standardisation according to the interviewees who support the approach.

The participants who substantiate personalisation mention in multiple occasions that good customised services encouraged them to purchase more frequently from the entity in question. This highlights two important facts.

Firstly, the quality of customer services not solely influences consumers' opinion about organisations, as Buzzell and Gale (1987) believe, but also that it enhances their loyalty. Payne et al. (1995), Lovelock and Wirtz (2004), Stewart (1997) and Oliver (1999) were then correct when they explained that customer services' quality greatly affects the generation of loyalty.

Secondly, a good use of personalisation is effective

at generating loyalty. This important observation is substantiated by the fact that no one among standardisation supporters talks about feeling loyal. This indicates that, although they are preferred by some consumers, good standardised services do not necessarily make them loyal while customisation does. Schieffer (2005), Oliver (1997, 1999) and Stewart (1997) all write extensively about the significance of loyalty in successful customer retention. Therefore, the findings suggest that standardisation is less effective at maintaining the clientele than customisation.

Moreover, the interviewees depict an extremely limited amount of standardised service examples. Resulting from this observation, a question arises: why do standardisation supporters not depict detailed examples of standardised services like customisation backers do? The answer lies in one participant's response:

"The majority of such interactions are average, and so don't stand out in everyday life" (M4).

These words summarise a heavy limitation of standardisation, which is also noted by Ritzer (2014) when describing McDonalidisation: standardisation produces an easily forgettable experience. This not solely implies a poor engagement of the customer but also diminishes the chance of rendering the client loyal, as the latter will not remember the service encounter even if it was satisfactory.

Furthermore, Woods et al (1986), Gudergan and Hoeck (2002) and Mörschel (2002) affirm that clearly structured standardised deliveries enable customers to distinguish easily companies that offer mediocre services form those that deliver good ones. Yet, if customers struggle to remember such experiences, then comparability is actually impossible and cannot be considered as a benefit of the approach. This fact also undermines the creation of loyalty.

Schuh (2000) praises standardisation for the equality and fairness it creates. Yet, M5 argues:

"I prefer the personalised way. Because I think as a customer, my problems are not the same as…as my neighbour's"

These words do not indicate that people expect equality. On the contrary, they highlight that individuals want to feel unique and special. Payne et al. affirm that "customers and their behaviour cannot be standardized" (1995, Pg.87), yet M5's words appear to imply that customers actually refuse to be standardised.

Yet, M1, a standardisation supporter, contrasts this observation:

"I am not a special person".

Therefore, it appears that some individuals want to be different and others prefer to stay hidden in the crowd. This drastic clash of views can be explained by the significant age gap, which separates M1 and M5. In fact, while the former is a student in his twenties who is only at the beginning of his life, M5 is a 70-year-old successful manager whose decades of experience definitely boosted his self-confidence.

Nonetheless, the contrasting views indicate that customers' do not all share the same opinion on the matter.

Yet, another participant, F5 praises a waitress for having brought her various teas to try before purchasing one. Being a typical feature of customisation, this example of preferential treatment first confirms that "customers tend to value the extra attention given to their needs" (Lovelock and Wirtz, 2004, Pg.370) and second, that several individuals want to feel unique.

F5 and M5 share the same need to feel special and interestingly they are a similar age. Possibly, an older age, with the broad variety of experiences it involves, increases people's self-confidence making them want to be treated differently and better than anyone else. If this is the case, agents can use this information in their best interest: when they deal with an elderly, for example, they may apply a customised approach knowing to exceed the customer's expectations.

In phone calls and face-to-face communications discerning the customer's age is rather easy. In written interactions, it is harder, yet the context, the discussed product/service, the query and the vocabulary can give hints.

Nevertheless, in response to objective 'b', the data shows that generally customisation generates loyalty more than standardisation, therefore personalised interactions are more effective at retaining customers than standardised communications.

HOW DO YOU LIKE IT?

CONCLUSIONS AND LIMITATIONS

The collection and analysis of primary data, combined with relevant theoretical notions, enabled the reaching of solid results in relations to two fundamental questions: a) how individuals prefer customer services to be delivered and b) which approach –customisation or standardisation- is more effective at retaining customers.

With regards to the first question, the findings of

this research demonstrate that consumers have precise expectations. They outline in detail how, from their perspective, agents should behave and deal with their queries.

In relation to the second question, it appears that individuals do not always favour the same approach. Their preferences depend on subjective and contextual factors.

Nevertheless, the data gathered illustrates that generally customisation is the most effective approach at generating loyalty, thus at maintaining the clientele.

Moreover, customisation appears to be the most popular approach. However, the divide is not striking and the chosen sample size is too restricted for a credible and reliable numerical argument.

Nonetheless, this limitation can be minimised or even eliminated in future studies by selecting a larger sample. In such a case, a sensible choice would be to apply a pragmatist methodology. Pragmatism lies in the middle of Morgan and Smirchich (1980)'s spectrum, thus between positivism and interpretivism. Accordingly, its goal is to "cross the divide between the quantitative and the qualitative" by mixing positivist and interpretivist methods (Curran and Blackburn, 2001, Pg.123). The result is a methodology where the "weaknesses of one paradigm can be offset with the strengths of the other" (Collis and Hussey, 2009, Pg.66). In fact, as this dissertation shows, the use of interpretivist methods allows a deep understanding of a social phenomenon. Yet, the inclusion of positivist elements would enable the production of accurate numerical observations and statistical analyses.

Moreover, it would diminish the limitations that arise from the exclusive adoption of interpretivism. This study highlights that bias always exists in the latter methodology: both interviews and thematic analysis rely completely on the researcher's interpretation, hence a significant margin of subjectivity influences the findings.

In summary, the result of a methodology mix would form a more comprehensive framework, the results of which would represent more robust and reliable foundations on which organisations may rely on. Although this research's conclusions represent valuable additions to marketing literature, providing businesses with useful and practical knowledge to better satisfy and retain their customers is this study's ultimate goal.

The findings underline the significance that customer services have gained in the modern world with regards to the generation of loyalty and subsequent consumer retention. Subsequently, it is of capital importance for businesses to provide their customer services agents with an adequate formation.

Nowadays, small and large entities make substantial investments on the improvement of their customer services. This dissertation's findings provide useful and priceless grounds on which businesses can elaborate successful training programs. This is particularly significant to small and new-born organisations, the means of which are more limited than large companies'.

Customer services' omnipresence in humans' lives

emphasise how studies on this topic are necessary: entities require further knowledge in order to maximise their clientele retention, thus increase their profits. Although several academics are continuously attempting to discover more, numerous other aspects of customer service delivery are still to be explored. This research is hoped not solely to be useful but also to stimulate the production of further studies.

HOW DO YOU LIKE IT?

BIBLIOGRAPHY

Arksey, H. Knight, P. (1999), Interviewing for Social Scientists, London: Sage

Bell, D. Deighton, J. Reinartz, W. Rust, R.T. Swartz, G.S. (2002), Seven Barriers to Customer Equity Management, Journal of Service Research, 5(1), Pg.77-85

Berry, L.L. (1983), Relationship Marketing. In Berry, L.L, Shostack, G.L. and Upah, G. Emerging Perspectives on Services Marketing, Pg.25-28, American Marketing Association

Blum U, Töpfer A, Eickhoff G, Jänchen I. (2001). Nutzen der Normung. In: DINMitteilungen 80 (5), Pg.350-361

Bolton, R.N. (1998), A dynamic model of the duration of the customer's relationship with a continuous service provider: The role of satisfaction, Marketing Science, 17(1), Pg.45-65

Boulding, W. Kalra, A. Staelin, R. (1999), The Quality Double Whammy, Marketing Science, 18(4), Pg.463-84

Boulding, W. Staelin, R. Ehret, M. Johnston, W.J. (2005), A CRM Roadmap: What We Know, Potential Pitfalls, and Where to Go, Journal of Marketing, 69 (4), Pg.155–166

Bowen, J. Ford, R.C. (2002), Managing Service Organizations: Does Having a "Thing" Make a Difference?, Journal of Management, 28 (3), Pg.447-469

Bowen, D.H. Siehl, C. Schneider, B. (1989), A Framework for Analyzing Customer Service Orientation in Manufacturing, Academy of Management Review, Vol.14, No.1, 75-95

Boyatzis, R. E. (1998). Transforming Qualitative Information: Thematic Analysis and Code Development. Thousand Oaks, CA: Sage.

Braun, V. Clarke, V. (2006), Using Thematic Analysis in Psychology. Qualitative Research in Psychology, 3 (2). Pg.77-101.

Buzzell, R.D. Gale, B.T. 1987, The PIMS Principles: Linking Strategy to Performance, Free Press.

Cant, M.C. Strydom, J.W. Jooste, C.J. (2009), Marketing Management, Juta&Company Ltd

Collis, J. Hussey, R. (2009), Business Research: A Practical guide for Undergraduate and Postgraduate Students, Third Edition, Palgrave Macmillian

Cook, S. (2010), Customer Care Excellence: How to Create an Effective Customer Focus, Kogan Page Publishers

Coolican, H.M. (1992), Research Methods and Statistics in Psychology, London: Hodder & Stoughton

Creswell, J.W. (1994), Research Design: Qualitative and Quantitative approaches, Thousand Oaks, CA: Sage

Creswell, J.W. (2003), Research Design: Qualitative and Quantitative approaches, Thousand Oaks, CA: Sage

Curran, J. Blackburn, R.A. (2001), Researching the Small Enterprise, London: Sage

Deighton, J.A. (1996), The Future of Interactive Marketing, Harvard Business Review 74, No.6 (November–December), Pg.151–160.

Dubois, P.L. Jolibert, A. Mühlbacher, H. (2007), Marketing management: A Value-Creation Process, Basingstoke, England, Pg.1-28

Easterby-Smith, M. Thorpe, R. Lowe, A. (1991), Management Research: An Introduction, London: Sage

Fogli, L. (2006), Customer Service Delivery: Research and Best Practices, John Wiley & Sons

Fornell, C. Wernerfelt, B. (1987), Defensive Marketing Strategy by Consumer Complaint Management, Journal of Marketing Research, 24 (November), Pg.337-46

Gounaris, S.P. Tzempelikos, N.P. Chatzpagiotou, K. (2007), The Relationships of Customer-Perceived Value, Satisfaction and Behavioural Intentions, Journal of Relationship Marketing, 6(1), Pg.63-87

Gounaris, S. Stathakopoulos, V. (2004). Antecedents and Consequences of Brand Loyalty: An Empirical Study, The Journal of Brand Management, Volume 11, Number 4, 1 April 2004, pp. 283-306(24)

Gronroos, C. (1990), Service Management and Marketing: Managing the Moments of Truth in Service Competition, Free Press/Lexington Books

Gronroos, C. (2000), Service Management and Marketing. A Customer Relationship Management Approach, John Wiley & Sons

Gudergan, G. and Hoeck, H. (2002), Dienstleistungs-Standards für globale Märkte, DIN-Fachbericht 116, Herausgeber: DIN Deutsches Institut für Normung e.V., Pg.16–36.

Gummeson, E. (1991), Qualitative Methods in Management Research, Newbury Park: Sage

Holloway, I. Todres, L. (2003). The Status of Method: flexibility, consistency and coherence. Qualitative Research, 3(3), 345-357.

Hooley, G. Piercy, N.F. Nicoulaud, B. (2008), Marketing Strategy and Competitive Positioning, 4th Edition, Harlow, UK, Prentice Hall, Pg.3-6

Kotler, P. Keller, K.L. Brady, M. Goodman, M. Hansen, T. (2009), Marketing Management, 1st European Edition, Pearson Education Limited

Lee, R.M. (1993), Doing Research on Sensitive Topics, London: Sage

Levitt, T. (1983), The Globalization of Markets, Harvard Business Review, May-June, Pg.92-102

Lovelock, C. Wirtz, J. (2004), Services Marketing: People, Technology, Strategy, Fifth Edition, Pearson Education Limited

Lovelock, C. Patterson, P. Wirtz, J. (2014), Services Marketing, Sixth Edition, Pearson Education Limited

Miles, M. B. Huberman, A. M. (1994). Qualitative data analysis: An expanded sourcebook (2nd ed.). Thousand Oaks, CA: Sage.

Morgan, R.M. Hunt, S.D. (1994), The Commitment-Trust Theory of Relationship Marketing, Journal of Marketing, 58(3), Pg.20-38

Morgan, G. Smirchich, L. (1980), The Case of Qualitative Research, Academy of Management Review, Vol. 5, Pg. 491-500

Mörschel, I. Behrens, H. Fähnrich, K. Elze, R. (2007). Standardisation in the Service Sector for Global Markets, In: Spath, D. Fähnrich, K. (2007), Advances in Services Innovations, Springer (Eds.)

Mörschel, I. (2002). Ein Referenzmodell zur Entwicklung von Dienstleistungs-Standards: Service Standards Engineering. In: DIN Deutsches Institut für Normung e. V. (2002): DIN-Fachbericht 116 „Standardisierung in der deutschen Dienstleistungswirtschaft – Potenziale und Handlungsbedarf". Beuth, Berlin, Pg.37-50

Normann, R. (1970), A Personal Quest for Methodology, Stockholm: Scandinavian Institute for Administrative Research

Oliver, R.L. (1997), Satisfaction: A Behavioural Respective on the Consumer, MacGraw-Hill

Oliver, R.L. (1999), Whence Consumer Loyalty?, Journal of Marketing, Vol.63, Pg.33-44

Payne A. Christopher M. Clark M. Peck H. (1995), Relationship Marketing—Key Concepts. Relationship Marketing for Competitive Advantage: Winning and Keeping Customers, Butterworth

Payne, A. Holt, S. (2001), Diagnosing Customer Value: Integrating the Value Process and Relationship Marketing, British Journal of Management, 12, Pg.159-82

Peppers, D. Rogers, M. (2005), Customers Don't Grow on Trees, Fast Company, July, Pg.25-6

Pine, J.B. Gilmore, J.H. (1999), The Experience Economy, Harvard Business School Press

Porter, M.E. 1980, Competitive Strategy, New York: Free Press

Prahalad, C.K. and Ramaswany, V. (2004), The Future of Competition: Co-Creating Unique Value with Customers, Harvard Business School Press

Ritzer, G. (2014), The McDonaldization of Society, 8th ed., Sage Publications

Reinartz, W. Thomas, J.S. Kumar, V. (2005), Balancing Acquisition and Retention Resources to Maximize Customer Profitability, Journal of Marketing, 69 (January), Pg.63-79

Robson, C. (1993), Real World Research: A Resource for Social Scientists and Practitioner Researchers, Oxford: Blackwell

Rubin, H. J., & Rubin, I. S. (1995). Qualitative interviewing: The art of hearing data. Thousand Oaks, CA: Sage.

Rust, R.T. Ambler, T. Carpenter, G.S. Kumar, V. Srivastava R.K. (2004), Measuring Marketing Productivity: Current Knowledge and Future Direction, Journal of Marketing, 68 (4), Pg.76–89.

Schieffer, R. (2005), Ten Key Consumer Insights, Thomson

Schmitt, B.H. (2000), Experiential Marketing: How to Get Customers to Sense, Feel, Think, Act, Relate, Simon and Schuster

Schneider, B. and White, S.S. (2004), Service Quality: Research Perspectives, SAGE Publications

Schuh, A. (2000), Global standardization as a success formula for marketing in Central Eastern Europe?, Journal of World Business, Vol.35, No. 6, Pg.133-148.

Shostack, G.L. (1985), Planning the Service Encounter, in Czepiel, J.A. Solomon, M.R. Suprenant, C.F. The Service Encounter, Lexington Books, Pg.243-54

Smith, D. (1998), Customer Service in the Utility Industry, 1998: Case Studies on Technology, Operations, and Billing and Payment Solutions, Chartwell, Inc.

Solomon, M.R. Suprenant, C. Czepiel, J.A. Gutman, E.G. (1985), A Role Theory perspective on Dyadic Interactions: The Service Encounter, Journal of Marketing, 49(Winter), Pg.99-111

Stewart, T.A. (1997), A Satisfied Customer Isn't Enough, Fortune, 136 (July 21), Pg.112-13

Taylor, G. W., & Ussher, J. M. (2001). Making sense of S&M: A discourse analytic account. Sexualities, 4(3), Pg.293-314.

Tiu Wright, L. Newman, A. Dennis, C. (2006), Enhancing Consumer Empowerment, European Journal of Marketing, 40(9/10), Pg.925-35

Van Maanen, J. (1983), Qualitative Methodology, London: Sage

Verman, L.C. (1973), Standardization, a New Discipline, Shoe String Press,

Vogt, W.P. (1993), Dictionary of Statistics and Methodology, Newbury Park, CA: Sage

Wallace, R.S.O. Mellor, C.J. (1988), Non-response Bias in Mail Accounting Surveys: A Pedagogical Note, British Accounting Review, Is. 20, Pg. 131-9

Webster, F.E. (1997), The Future Role of Marketing in the Organisation, in Lehmann, D.R. Jocz, K.E. (eds.), Reflections on the Futures of Marketing, Marketing Science Institute

Weinstein, A. (2012), Superior Customer Value: Strategies for Winning and Retaining Customers, Third Edition, CRC Press

Woods, A. Fletcher, P. Hughes, A. (1986). Statistics in Language Studies, Cambridge University Press

Zeithaml, V.A. (2000), Service Quality, Profitability, and the Economic Worth of Customers: What We Know and What We Need to Learn, Journal of the Academy of Marketing Science, 28 (67), Pg.67-85

Zeithaml, Valarie A. (1988). Consumer Perceptions of Price, Quality, and Value: A Means-End Model and Synthesis of Evidence. Journal of Marketing 52 (July): Pg.2-22.

APPENDICES

App.1: Interview Prepared Questions

1. In general, what is the main reason (or reasons) that pushes you to contact customer services?

2. Overall, as a customer, how has your experience with customer services been so far?

3. Did you have particularly negative experiences?

4. What factors made the experience particularly bad?

5. Did you have particularly positive experiences?

6. What factors made the experience particularly good?

7. When remembering your last customer

service experience, do you remember the tone, vocabulary and attitude of the agent?

8. Was his approached personalized to your needs and if so how?

9. Do the effectiveness and quality of customer services influence your opinion of the organisation you are dealing with?

10. Do the effectiveness and quality of customer services affect your purchase choice?

11. Do you select a product or service also on the basis of the quality of customer services?

12. Do you generally deal again with a company that provided you with a bad customer service?

13. Do you prefer dealing with a company that offers a good customer service although it might be more costly that the alternatives?

14. If you were to give advice to agents, what in your opinion are the unacceptable mistakes that should be avoided in a delivery?

15. Generally, if you were to give advice to customer services agents, what in your opinion would make a delivery excellent?

App.2 Interviews Examples

Example 1

INTERVIEWEE	F2
GENDER	Female
NATIONALITY	Italian
AGE	30
PROFESSION	Marketing Quality Analyst

-Introduction-
Researcher (Re): this interview is recorded obviously but it will remain anonymous. However, I will have to ask you for some demographics, which will be used only for quality and research purposes within an academic environment. Do you agree?
Interviewee (Int): I agree.
Re: Perfect. I'm going to start with a small iteration.
This interview is about customer services and their deliveries. What is considered as customer service is very broad: from face-to-face encounters, to communications over the phone to written interactions like live chats or email.
I will ask you a range of questions about your experiences. In your answers you may use examples of companies and state their names if you wish or keep them anonymous.
Int: Ok.
-Interview-

Re: In general, what is the main reason or reasons that push you to contact customer services?

Int: If I have a problem that needs sorting.

Re: Hmm...Are there any other reasons?
Int: …..not really.

Re: Very well. Overall, as a customer, how has your ex-perience with customer services been so far?

Int: Hmm…Up and down.

Re: Did you have any particularly negative experiences?

Int: Hmm… fairly recently, yes. When I had my broadband installed. The equipment had to be connected. Hmmm….I went through the customer service of course to organise and arranged an appointment. Hmm…it was arranged for one morning, one Monday morning…hmm…and the engineer was supposed to turn up at 8 'clock. He never did. Hmm…He said to the company that he was there at 8 o'clock knocking on the door and he left a card. And this is not true because I was there until 8:45. Nobody knocked on the door. And since I live in a block of flats he wouldn't have been able to my get to my door because he would have had to ring the main door bell. So, I placed a formal complaint with the company, who contacted me back and said they were looking into it.
…And they kept me updated on the progress. Unfortunately, I had to wait for another two weeks until the engineer came out again!! …And, yeah, the complaints department was

actually…the lady was very nice and she kept in touch with me with the pro-gress of it. However, the actual main office was always on the side of the engineer. So in the end we got it sorted. The engineer was late to the second appointment as well but it got sorted.

Re: Concerning the first communication with this company, was it face-to-face?

Int: No. It was all done over the phone.

Re: You mentioned…timing problems. Is timing something you really consider when judging customer services?

Int: Yes, absolutely. If they say that something is gonna be done at a certain time, and that's what I expect. I'm paying for that service and that's the service I expect to receive.

Re: Through your answer, you also involve the concept of missed promise. Is it also something that really affects your judgement?

Int: Absolutely. I am be pretty unhappy if if someone or something was supposed to be doing something and it's not been done.

Re: Very well. Hmm…You talked also about a lady from another department who was very nice. In what way was she nice?

Int: Hmm...She promised to look into the problem and she kept me updated and it was true. She actually kept her word and she kept me updated with emails and phone calls, and left messages, voicemail messages if she couldn't reach me...hmm...and she did her best to sort the problem.

Re: Very well. Are there other factors that made the experience particularly bad?

Int: Hmm...The fact that they were more on the side of the en-gineer rather than the customer. Well, you would have thought since we are the ones paying, they would have been more...hmm...helpful. They weren't very helpful. They were like, "Oh, well the engineer said..." Hmm...Well, the engineer never did what he said. So yes, that's another problem. They're not on the side of the customer.

Re: Very well. Did you have any particularly positive expe-riences?

Int: Hmm...I suppose...I don't know. I called to enquire about...hmm...some electricity quotes and some energy suppliers. Err...I called energy suppliers to get some quotes and one particular company was quite good. The agent was very friendly and very nice, very helpful. He explained the de-tails, answered all my questions. Nothing to complain about, but it's nothing outstanding either.

Re: When remembering your last customer service experience do you remember the tone, vocabulary and attitude of the agent?

Int: Not particularly. His tone was friendly…hmm…he was up-beat…hmm…I can't remember his vocabulary to be honest.

Re: Hmm…when you say his tone was upbeat, in what ways?

Int: Well, he wasn't like…he didn't sound bored or anything like that. He was like, actually really friendly and…He didn't sound like he was falling asleep or bored out of his mind like some of the agents do.

Re: Fair enough, always about your last customer service experience, was his approach personalised to your needs?

Int: Yes. He asked the questions about the place where I was living. So as to make it…as to provide the best quote that he could…err…that he could offer for the company…hmm…he advised me against certain plans because he said they wouldn't be worth in your case and so, yes, he was personalised in that sense. He tried to build a rapport with me.

Re: And did you like it?

Int: Yes.

Re: Do you prefer when they try to build a rapport with you or would you rather go for a standard procedure by the customer service?

Int: It depends on the situation like, if I'm in the rush I don't really care of them building a rapport. I just want them to get whatever I want done. Hmm...In some other instances, it's fine.

Re: Fair enough. Do the effectiveness and quality of customer services influence your opinion on the organisation you're dealing with?

Int: Yes, absolutely. If I received bad customer service from a company, well, I'm very likely not to go back and use their services or use their products anymore.

Re: Hmmm...So, would you say that the effectiveness and quality of customer services affect your purchase choice?

Int: Yes, absolutely.

Re: Do you select a product of service also on the basis of the quality of customer services?

Int: Yes. If I had previous positive experiences, I'm more likely to go back to that company or to that product.

Re: Would you prefer dealing with the company that offers a good customer service although it might be more costly than the alternatives?

Int: Depending on the company, yes. Depending on what the service is. For instance, if it's an insurance company for instance, say. I read reviews online that they're terrible to deal with. If you need to make a claim, I wouldn't go for that because that's what's an insurance company are meant to do. And chances are, that if something happens and I need to do a cl-, to make a claim, I want my money quickly. But if the customer service is terrible, there's no chance of that. So I'd rather pay a bit more but be sure.

Re: Ok, do you generally deal again with a company that provided you with a bad customer service?

Int: No, unless I have no choice. For instance, when I mentioned about the broadband, I had no choice but to use that one per contract.

Re: So would you say that that the company retained you as a customer more out of inertia and lack of choice than preference?

Int: Absolutely.

Re: Very well. If you were to give advice to agents, what in your opinion are the unacceptable mistakes that should be avoided in the delivery?

Int: Hmm…Being rude. So…hmm…sounding bored, sounding aggres-sive, antagonising. Hmm…sounding uninterested like, you say something and they completely ignore it. That's not good.

Re: Any other?

Int: Well, yeah of course….they need to try and solve the problem. And if they can't…hmm…to try and find someone who can sort it out.

Re: When you say "rude', what do you mean by that?

Int: Hmm…I suppose…hmm…not saying "please", "thank you" and being impolite in that way. Interrupting you…hmm…the tone of their voice, if it doesn't sound…hmm…if it doesn't sound friendly.

Re: How do they sound bored? How do they sound uninterested?

Int: Hmm…well, if their tone is like flat…ok…alright. Very transactional. Like when someone for instance is reading "terms and conditions" for instance. Then that's all… all flat. If they're interested in you, they ask questions but they got a certain tone to it. I don't know how to explain it to be honest.

Re: Do you pay attention to the vocabulary?

Int: Yes. I mean, if an agent sounds very vague like, "I don't know, I'm not sure", things like that, then obviously that reflects…that gives an impression of not be-ing…hmm…connected. It makes me feel…not particularly good to be honest and I'm like, "why am I wasting my time with you"?

Re: Generally, if you were to give advice to customer ser-vices agents, hmm…what in your opinion would make a delivery excellent?

Int: Well, the opposite of what I mentioned. So being friendly, being upbeat, being interested in what a customer is saying, paying attention, trying to solve the prob-lem…hmm…things like that really…..obviously using a positive vocabulary since we've mentioned vocabulary…hmm…positive words…hmm…

Re: By "positive words" what do you mean?

Int: Positive words, I don't know, something that…like good….Like, if an agent says, "Oh!

This is a good plan for you. This is a perfect plan for you", based on your needs, things like that. So he emphasises...hmm...the good points.

Re: So you said "based on your needs", which implies a cer-tain degree of personalisation of the delivery to the indi-vidual customer service agent. Would you advise customer services to be trained on a degree of personalisation?

Int: Yes. We need to identify the customer's needs to pro-vide the best service possible. So, we need to find out what the customer wants...hmm... what customer is after and then based on that, provide the service or products that are re-quired. They also need to use the right words and try to...hmm...try to discover and find out the informations from the customer. They can't just...Otherwise, they could come across as rude if they are too direct at them. Building a rapport is essential and from there asking questions.

Re: Your words were "building a rapport is essential". Thus you would not appreciate a standardised customer service de-livery if you were a customer in need?

Int: Generally no. But you talked about customer service in a broad way. Therefore, I'm thinking for instance when I go to the supermarket at the till and there's a cashier that asks, "How was your day?", and things like that. And that really, I couldn't do that ah ah [laughing]. That is simply useless and superfluous.

Re: In which cases do you think it is really useful?

Int: It is useful on certain…hmm…in certain fields of customer service.

Re: Could you give an example?

Int: When they need to provide a specific product or they need to provide specific services but, I suppose a cashier is providing customer service but she's not providing really products or services. She is just doing her job like, scanning the items.

Re: Ok. Hmm… lastly…hmm…do you ever have like, a friendly chat for example with a waiter at the restaurant or in a pub?

Int: Not normally….Sometimes but not often. if I'm in a rush and stuff, I don't appreciate that. If I have some spare time and I'm in a fairly good mood then that is fine. If you can ask, "How's the weather?", and banalities like that.

Re: And in written communications what would you advise to agent in order to sound friendly?

Int: I would say opening pleasantries, closing

> *pleasantries...err...using positive words throughout the communication. Hmm...that it's a harder situation I suppose. I never really thought about it.*

Re: Hmm...Do you...do you notice for example vocabulary or spelling or grammatical mistakes?

> *Int: Yeah. Absolutely. That annoys me. That really annoys me and I don't think it's very professional when it's not grammatically correct...hmm...and there's like, not even a syntax and things like that. So, it needs to be right.*

Re: Very well. And in your experiences have you noticed if the agents actually use your name?

> *Int: Hmmm...yes, generally speaking, yes. In the few communications that I had by email they usually do use my name.*

Re: Also in verbal communications, like vocal?

> *Int: Hmm...Not so much there because my name is harder to pronounce for them. So, I don't really mind if they don't, rather than them pronouncing it incorrectly. So...*

Re: Do you like when they use it?

> *Int: Hmm...It doesn't really affect me to be honest.*

-End of Interview-
Example 2

INTERVIEWEE	M3
GENDER	Male
NATIONALITY	German
AGE	47
PROFESSION	Real Estate Photographe

-Introduction-
Researcher (Re): this interview is recorded obviously but it will remain anonymous. However, I will have to ask you for some demographics, which will be used only for quality and research purposes within an academic environment. Do you agree?
Interviewee (Int): I agree.
Re: Perfect. I'm going to start with a small iteration.
This interview is about customer services and their deliveries. What is considered as customer service is very broad: from face-to-face encoun-ters, to communications over the phone to written interactions like live chats or email.
I will ask you a range of questions about your experiences. In your an-swers you may use examples of companies and state their names if you wish or keep them anonymous.
Int: Ok.

-Interview-
Re: In general, what is the main reason (or reasons) that pushes you to contact customer services?

Int: I don't contact customer services very often. I try to avoid them as much as possible. We live in a world dominated by information. It's so easy to find information nowadays. I use the internet most of time to resolve my problems. Still, if I really cannot find a solution myself, I will contact customer services.

Re: So the main reason that pushes you to contact customer services is issues, correct?

Int: Yes. Issues.

Re: I see. Overall, as a customer, how has your experience with customer services been so far?

Int: Good and bad. I had bad experiences and good ones. Gen-erally I noticed that customer services in Germany are much more efficient and proactive than in the UK. In Germany, what matters is finding the solution. Here in the UK I no-ticed that agents waste a lot of time with irrelevant blath-ering and useless chats which only make me waste my time and patience.

Re: Oh, so did you have particularly negative experiences?

Int: Well…yeah. I mean most of the time customer services are not too bad. But they're not excellent either. Actually, they're far from been excellent. The worst experience was probably with Ryanair. I booked two tickets for me and my partner to go to Berlin. I filled out the form as usual online but I was very busy when I was do-ing it. My partner's called Daniel and by mistake I wrote on the form Danier. It was a typo, it happens to everybody to make these small mistakes. So I looked for the way to amend this on the webpage. I found it and wrote the name correct-ly. I was saving when a message popped up saying that I needed to pay 112 Pounds to change the name! I was absolutely furious. This is not acceptable. This is the worst way to keep a customer happy. So I called the customer services. After 8 minutes and a half and about 4 Pounds wasted, I fi-nally managed to talk to a human being. I explained my prob-lem calmly at first but the man would not allow me to change the typo for free. He said that changing the passenger on a plane is something that needs to be charged. I was getting even more furious! I didn't want to change the bloody pas-senger, but only correct a typo!!! So I began to be extreme-ly upset and as I was complaining the agent hung up on me!!! Absolutely unacceptable. The company should be ashamed. It treats people like cattle! So I wrote a serious email to the headquarters, threatening to make a scandal on social media. After two hours I received a very formal and polite reply affirming that the mistake had been corrected free of charge….Now luckily my problem was solved, but it took me money, time and energy. A horrible experience. An agent that hangs up on the customer!!! Unbelievable. This would never happen in Germany!

Re: What factors exactly made the experience particularly bad?

Int: First of all the rudeness. It is not acceptable to

hang up the phone for example. Also, the agent's tone was ex-tremely unfriendly. He sounded bored and irritated at me. The words he used were also rude. At some point he told me 'Sir, I'm afraid I cannot make this amendment without charg-ing you. It is your responsibility to pay attention to what you are doing. Not mine.'…..How can anyone dare to treat like this a stranger, a client?! There used to be the famous principle of 'the customer is always right'. Where did it end up?

Then of course the timing was not good. 8 minutes and 30 seconds of hold just to get someone to talk to is way too much. Even if I had not been angry already, I would have be-come it anyway during the wait.

Re: I see, and did you have particularly positive experienc-es?

Int: As I already said, exceptional experiences are a rari-ty. I do not think I've had exceptional ones. I did have some decent ones though. Yesterday I went to the camera shop on high street. I needed to buy a new bag for my new Nikon. Foolishly I had forgotten my tele zoom at home –my biggest lens- and could not be sure if my camera and the lens would have fitted in the bags I was looking at. The lady under-stood my doubts before I had even spoken and gave me similar zoom so that I could try to see it the bags were big enough. I appreciated it very much.

Re: What factors made the experience particularly good?

> *Int: The lady anticipated my needs in a very thoughtful and polite manner. She had a good....selling behaviour. I mean, it was clear that she wanted to help and sell and she managed. I did buy in the end. She was very nice. She smiled a lot. She was also very pretty and young.*

Re: Ah ah (laughing). Has the fact that the agent was good-looking enhanced your experience?

> *Int: …Well, the politically correct answer would be no, it has not ah ah (laughing).*

Re: And the honest answer?

> *Int: Ah ah (laughing)…yes it did! I mean, the main point is that she was efficient and fast at her job. She helped me with what I needed in a professional way. The fact that she looked nice and had a sweet smile was the cherry on top. After all, I am a man and pretty ladies have an impact on me.*
> *For example, I accepted to be interviewed by you because I liked the idea of contributing to research. But the fact that you asked in a kind a way and that you're pretty convinced me straight away ah ah (laughing)!*

Re: Ah ah (laughing), thanks for the compliment and for accepting to be interviewed. Moving on, when remembering your last customer service experience, do you remember the tone, vocabulary and attitude of the agent?

Int: Eeeer………….I bought the ticket this morning on the bus. Obviously the exchange was very brief but I remember that the driver was in a very good mood despite the time. Ah ah (laughing)…it was 6.45 in the morning, generally no one is in happy at that time!

Re: Very true! And was his approached personalized to your needs and if so how?

Int: Eh…well, I wouldn't say that. We didn't really speak that much….Well actually in a way it was, he was smiley and when I got off the bus he wished me a good day at work.

Re: And did you like this comment?

Int: Yes I did. I found it very polite and thoughtful. Generally I hate when customer services try to be extremely friendly because it sounds fake. And I don't like when they use personal information about me to have a conversation with me.

Re: so you do not appreciate that customer services personalize their deliveries to you specifically, correct?

Int: Exactly. I found it highly disrespectful and time consuming. A good service should always follow a standard procedure based on effectiveness and rapidity. Now, a small friendly comment like the driver's can be nice. Also the use of the first name is welcome. I like it. But no more than that.

Re: I see. Again, generally, do the effectiveness and quality of customer services influence your opinion of the organisation you are dealing with?

Int: Absolutely. Customer services are an important part of a business and are often the main tools to sell more. When I see good customer services, I feel safer, I trust the company more.

Re: And do the effectiveness and quality of customer ser-vices affect your purchase choice?

Int: Customer services can be good and make me buy. An exa-ple is the lady at the photography store. She was effective and in the end I bought. Obviously, it's not only the customer services that encourage me to purchase. There are also other factors like the price, the quality, my finances and needs…and more.

However, I write down the companies that I like according to some criteria. Customer services are one of these criteria and if I'm pleased I will buy from them again.

Re: So do you select a product or service also on the basis of the quality of customer services?

Int: Yes I do.

Re: Do you generally deal again with a company that provided you with a bad customer service?

Int: If the business dissatisfied me deeply, then I won't be their customer anymore. I also write down on a black list the companies I dislike. If they made a mistake and offer me some kind of compensation, then I will think about it. Plus, sometimes there's no choice. I can't change certain business deals. For example, I hate Southwest Waters. They're the most expensive water suppliers of the country and when I called them to get some information, their customer services were not the best. Still, I need water so I can't really do that much about it, even 'though I'm not satisfied with the company at all.

Re: Do you prefer dealing with a company that offers a good customer service although it might be more costly that the alternatives?

Int: Generally yes. The extra money is almost always worth the safety. I don't like problems, you see? I'm a busy man, I have no time to waste. If I need something, I want it fast and working. If this involves more money, I'll pay cause it will save me time which to me is money.

Re: Excellent. If you were to give advice to agents, what in your opinion are the unacceptable mistakes that should be avoided in a delivery?

Int: The unacceptable mistakes....I have a full list!

Re: Could you expand on that?

Int: Slow, not listening to the customer, not keeping promises, rudeness, not smiling, not offering help, not demonstrating the willingness to sell, fake friendliness, language mistakes.....

Re: By language mistakes, what do you mean?

Int: Well errors in declinations, in German for example, or wrong uses of verbs....or spelling errors, grammatical errors in emails...They are unprofessional. They give the impression that the company doesn't care at all about customers... They are a symbol of disrespect.

Re: Generally, if you were to give advice to customer ser-vices agents, what in your opinion would make a delivery excellent?

Int: The opposite of what I said before really: Rapidity, efficiency, listening, accurate language, politeness without exaggeration, an attitude to sell and help....these really...oh, keeping promises is very important too. If agents promise to call me back or to do something for me, then they must do it and within the timeframe they gave. They must also be precise. We are busy people, we have lives and commitments. Agents must understand that and give precise information so we can organize ourselves. Also showing empathy is crucial, especially with complaints. Saying sorry, admitting the fault or error and finding an alternative solution immediately is the best way to satisfy an angry customer.

Re: Absolutely. When you say politeness and rudeness, what do you mean exactly?

Int: By rudeness I mean everything that is not polite obviously ah ah (laughing). So…aggressive speech, lack of 'please' and 'thank you'…..eeeh…interruptions…swear words.. By politeness, I mean educated speech, gentle words, a smiley tone of voice, enthusiasm…

Re: And in written communications, how can politeness be shown?

Int: By writing without making mistakes of any kind, by avoiding bad words and using the standard greetings and sign offs…..Eeeehm….that's it really….it's not that difficult.

-End of Interview-

HOW DO YOU LIKE IT?

App.3 Example of coded transcript

73

Reasons for contacting: ISSUE

Re: In general, what is the main reason (or reasons) that pushes you to contact customer services?

Int: Well, I'd say that in general I call because of an issue. If I have a problem with a company, instead of driving myself crazy to find a solution, I call the customer services. Now.... it's also true that it depends on the company. I tend to call to get information about something, like some time ago when I wanted to know when sales would start in a clothing shop.

Reasons for contacting: INFORMATION

Re: I see, so you contact customer services mainly if you have issues or need information, is that correct?

Int: Indeed, I can't think of any other reasons really...

Re: You mentioned that you call customer services. Do you favour calling rather than having a face to face interaction or emailing or chatting?

Way to contact: CALL

Int: Hmmm...yes, generally speaking I tend to call customer services but it depends. Depending on the context, sometimes I go to speak, personally. Last week for example I was at the train station, I wasn't sure which platform was my train on, so I just asked personally.

Way to contact: PERSONALLY

Re: Of course.

Way to contact: CALL (reasons)

Int: But otherwise, I prefer to call. I don't feel like writing about my problem, especially if it is a long one to explain. Uff...I get back from work very tired. Really don't feel like writing an A4 page to explain. Plus, I kind of prefer to talk to someone. Like this, I can make sure my query is actually understood and generally it's also quicker because I don't have to wait for a reply to arrive.

Way to contact: PERSONALLY (reasons)

TIMING **UNDERSTANDING/LISTENING**

Re: Very well, and do you contact customer services often?

HABIT OF CONTACTING CS

Int: Well....I'd say yes, quite often. Then, of course, it depends on times of the year. Before Christmas, it's more likely that I will cause I buy a lot.

Re: Fair enough. And overall, as a customer, how has your experience with customer services been so far?

Point of overall agreement: VARIED EXPERIENCE

Int: Oh well... ah ah ah (laughing)...very very varied! I saw them all! I've been treated wonderfully by some and was deeply offended by others!

Re: Well, since you mention it, did you have particularly negative experiences?

Object of call: CALL

Int: Oh yeah! Several! Like a month ago with Apple! I called them because I wanted to have an idea of what are the differences between an Iphone 6 and a 6s and the lady kept on asking me for a...hmm, a serial number I guess. Hmm...I kept telling her that I didn't have one. I mean, I could NOT have one since I hadn't even bought the bloody thing yet! But she would just not listen, and at the end she said that she could not help me because I wasn't a customer! Can you believe that?! My husband called them back a couple days later and he spoke apparently to a really nice guy who explained everything very nicely. So yes, the lady could have actually helped me!

NEG. experiences
LISTENING
NOT HELPFUL

Re: This is very interesting! What factors specifically made the experience particularly bad?

Important!
→ Rudeness is remembered

150

HOW DO YOU LIKE IT?

[margin: LISTENING / NOT HELPFUL / RUDENESS]

Int: Well, obviously the fact that she wasn't listening to me at all. I mean, she truly ignored what I was saying. And also her refusal to help me while I'm calling to get some info to buy a product! I mean, the lady clearly didn't want to work. Plus, at times, she was also rude.

Re: I see. In what ways was she rude?

[margin: RUDENESS / TONE / NOT HELPFUL]

Int: Her tone, for one, was absolutely harsh! She was interrupting me and always saying that she could not do this, could not help and stuff. She was very negative and from her attitude and language, you could clearly feel she just wanted to hang up and not work.

[margin: ATTITUDE / LANGUAGE]

Re: How was her language?

[margin: LANGUAGE / TONE / KNOWLEDGE / FALSE FRIENDLINESS]

Int: Negative mainly. She was only using negations: 'I cannot', 'I'm not able', 'I can't help'... sentences like this. And she had a very annoying tone of voice. A fake friendly tone which tried to hide in vain her lack of kindness... A awful experience and a waste of time for me cause I didn't even get the answer I needed!

Re: Interesting! And did you have particularly positive experiences?

[margin: Important / VARIED EXPERIENCE]

Int: Yes indeed, I must say that on average I was treated well. There were some bad experiences like the one I just told you about, but overall, the level is quite good. I must admit, the exceptional experiences, though are rare, much more than the bad ones. Still, there are a few.

Re: Could you give an example? **[annotation: hesitation to think of a positive exp. No hesitation for negative.]**

Int: Hmmm... let me think... hum... oh well there is that one time when I had bought a camera from Amazon. The camera arrived and worked. Still, it was an expensive one with a great reputation as well and I had the impression there was something wrong with mine because the quality of videos was not... that good.

[margin: Way to contact / CHAT]

So... I contacted Amazon straight away, by chat. That's the only time I've ever used chats by the way. And the man or woman sent me immediately a return label and made sure a new camera would be dispatched to me. All this without forcing me to complain for hours. It was quick and easy, a matter

[margin: TIMING]

of a couple of minutes.

Re: Excellent then! And what factors exactly made the experience particularly good?

[margin: TIMING / UNDERSTANDING / LISTENING / ATTITUDE/TONE / LANGUAGE]

Int: As I said, it was quick and very easy. You know, the agent was very effective, did not waste my time and understood my problem immediately. Also, the attitude of the agent was exceptional! I mean, we only exchanged a few sentences, but these were great! He or she was very kind and helpful. For example, after I had explained my problem, the agent said something along the lines of 'I see, madam. Do not worry, we will resolve this straight away'... something like this. It was very professional. And at the end of the chat, the agent personalized the conversation and said something like 'I'm sure you'll now be

[margin: Personalisation]

able to make astonishing videos with the new camera'. It was a great experience and I bought again

[margin: Important]

with Amazon because I know I can trust them.

[annotation: → C.S. engenders TRUST]

Re: Would you say you're a loyal customer with regards to Amazon?

Int: Yeah... yes, absolutely.

[annotation: C.S. engenders [LOYALTY] but it's not enough ⇒ C.S. contributes to LOYALTY]

HOW DO YOU LIKE IT?

[Margin note: 3]

Re: Is your loyalty due to their effective customer services?

[Margin note: Important / Loyalty]

Int: Well... Not only. I like the company in general and their products too. They have a bit of everything, they have a good website, they dispatch almost everywhere and they're quite safe with payments. But yeah, their good customer services definitely encourage me more to buy form them for sure, especially quite pricey objects where trust matters more.

Re: When remembering your last customer service experience, do you remember the tone, vocabulary and attitude of the agent?

Int: Hmmm, let me think.... supermarkets count right?

Re: Yes, indeed.

[Margin note: RUDENESS]

Int: Well yesterday I went with my husband to do the weekly shopping at Tesco. As usual, the lady at the till was quite impolite... *[annotation: (Important) → Rudeness is remembered]*

Re: In what way?

[Margin note: RUDENESS / ATTITUDE/TONE]

Int: She was talking mainly to her colleague. We couldn't even understand at times if she was asking us questions or continuing her conversation with her friend! She never looked at us or smiled or anything... she didn't even say 'hello' or 'goodbye'. Yes, generally her attitude was quite rude.

Re: So, you wouldn't say her approach was personalised to your needs?

Int: Well obviously not! But it wasn't even a standard approach either. Basically there was no approach at all (laughing)! The lady didn't interact with us at all! Next time we'll go to the automatic tills.

Re: I see. Going back to a general scale, do the effectiveness and quality of customer services influence your opinion of the organisation you are dealing with?

[Margin note: Important / conditions affect her]

Int: Yes, absolutely. As I mentioned before, while talking about Amazon, I regard a company differently if I'm well treated and vice versa. After all, customer services are the façade of a business, thus it's obvious that they will affect my opinion. It's also true, though, that I never really dealt with the customer services of many companies. For example, I'm absolutely crazy about Ralph Lauren clothing. Yet I cannot really afford buying this kind of items at their official stores. I just go to outlets or vintage shops. So, yes, I'm absolutely loyal to Ralph Lauren in the sense that I love their clothes, their style and their quality. I mean I'm still wearing pull overs that I bought ten years ago and they're still perfect. But I wouldn't know if their customer services were good enough. Never had the need to contact them directly.

Re: Do the effectiveness and quality of customer services affect your purchase choice?

[Margin note: C.S. affect her opinion but it depends]

Int: Generally, I'd say yes, but it depends on what I'm purchasing really. Sometimes I call customer services to ask for information about something. If they answer me well, then yes I will feel safer and will probably buy as well. Still, if they are not extremely good, I won't choose to buy or not to buy just because of that. If I want something badly, bad customer services won't stop me. For example, even though I was treated horribly by the Apple lady, I still bought an Iphone 6s for my son's birthday.

HOW DO YOU LIKE IT?

[Margin note: 4]
[Margin note: C.S. effect but opinion, it depends]

Re: Do you select a product or service also on the basis of the quality of customer services?

Int: Hmmm...that's a tricky question....I'd say yes and no. Like...it depends...

Re: On what does it depend?

[Margin notes: important; C.S. important when buying; C.S. effect but middle, it depends]

Int: Well, for example with Amazon, now that I know that their customer services are quick and do their job properly, I tend to buy from there more. Especially when it comes to important purchases, like the camera, I feel much safer if I buy with them. At the same time, I don't always know how the customer services of a company are and generally I don't really think of investigating before buying, particularly if it is a small thing.
So, to answer your question, yes.... customer services do matter when I already know how they are and mainly when I'm buying something costly. Otherwise, I don't really think about them.

Re: Do you generally deal again with a company that provided you with a bad customer service?

[Margin note: BRAND INERTIA]

Int: I try not to ah ah (laughing)! But sometimes it's just not possible. For example, I hate my bank and the customer services are useless. Still, changing would be a big hassle which honestly I'm not prepared to face. I'm lazy and that makes me loyal. ...Nevertheless, I tend to give more than one chance to customer services. I was treated badly by Apple but, when my husband called and another agent answered, he was treated very politely apparently. So I do not feel like condemning a company just because one of their employees is incompetent..

[Margin note: ONE MORE CHANCE TO CS]

Re: I understand. Do you prefer dealing with a company that offers a good customer service although it might be more costly that the alternatives?

[Margin note: SPENDING EXTRA for GOOD CS (relate this to secondary data)]

Int: Ah...that's a good question! Well sometimes I search products I've seen on Amazon on Ebay. Generally they're a bit cheaper on Ebay. If I'm buying something pricey, I still go for Amazon even though it could be even more expensive, in mind is worth the extra money. However, if I'm buying something that is already quite cheap, like no more than 30/40 Pounds and there is a significant price difference between Amazon and Ebay, then I will go for Ebay. The risk will not be huge even if I have difficulties.

Re: Ok. If you were to give advice to agents, what in your opinion are the unacceptable mistakes that should be avoided in a delivery?

[Margin notes: TIMING; LISTENING; RUDENESS; TONE; FAKE FRIENDLINESS; PROMISE KEEPING]

Int: Well, timing is extremely important. Agents should learn how to be quick but very often they take ages. Then, listening carefully to the customer is also vital. So many times I had to explain once again my problem because the person was not listening to me.... That's irritating, tedious and also wastes time. They should avoid rudeness both in terms of vocabulary and of attitude. Sometimes agents use polite words and sentences but their behaviour shows the contrary. I hate this kind of...fake friendliness.
Also, maintaining promises is crucial. A few months ago I had called my bank because I couldn't log onto my online account. I called their customer services and the lady told me she would call me back within 3 hours. She never did and I had to call back. Now, this is not acceptable! If you're promising something, keep it. Otherwise, don't promise anything!

153

HOW DO YOU LIKE IT?

[Margin note: LISTENING]
[Margin note: TIMING]
[Margin note: important]
[Margin note: Personalisation]

Re: Very well. Generally, if you were to give advice to customer services agents, what in your opinion would make a delivery excellent?

Int: Well…as I said, I think that the most important thing agents should focus on is listening. Most of the time agents don't understand the query and so you're forced to explain again, which is tedious and time-consuming. And timing is also important. Customer services should be quick because people are busy. Now, of course, a friendly chat can be nice but often agents don't understand if the customer is in the mood or is in a rush.

[Margin note: Personalisation]
[Margin note: important]

Re: When you say a friendly chat, what do you mean exactly?

Int: Well, you know, when they start having a conversation with you which is a bit more…personal. I like that. I like when they personalize the conversation. It makes me feel…unique, you know. It's a bit like when they use your name a lot. I like the fact that they remember it and use it. It's very friendly and kind. But sometimes I just don't have time and they should understand that there is no point in keeping me on the phone. At the end of the day I simply want my issue to be resolved.

Re: And how should their tone and vocabulary be?

[Margin note: LANGUAGE]
[Margin note: TONE]

Int: Well, first of all, I hate when they use jargon. Sometimes agents use very specific words, which to them working in that sector are daily language, but to us common mortals they do not mean anything at all, ah ah (laughing)! I hate it, it makes me feel silly and does not help me with my problem. When it comes to tone, agents should smile, be friendly, patient and polite at all times.

Re: I see and, in your opinion, how are politeness and friendliness conveyed in a written communication?

[Margin note: WRITTEN LANGUAGE]

Int: That's definitely harder. As I said, my experience with emails and live chats is very limited. However, I think the best way to show politeness is by writing a structured text with a good greeting and sign off and perhaps by using enthusiastic words.

Re: What do you mean by enthusiastic words?

[Margin note: LANGUAGE]

Int: Well, you know…words like 'have a great day' or 'I hope you'll be pleased with your purchase', 'it's an excellent choice'…things like that really.

Re: Very interesting. And remaining in the area of written communications, do spelling and grammar mistakes affect your judgment?

[Margin note: SPELLING ERRORS]

Int: It happened to me to spot errors. Generally speaking, I'd say they bother me. Now, with internet and checkers it is so easy to avoid mistakes! But it's also true that, as long as the errors are not too big, there's a limit to how much I care about them. It would be best if they were avoided, don't misunderstand me. Mistakes are not very professional. But, at the same time, I mainly want my query to be resolved so I can close my eyes on certain mistakes. We all make them out of tiredness or distraction.

154

HOW DO YOU LIKE IT?

ABOUT THE AUTHOR

Born in Paris, France, Victoria spent the majority of her upbringing in Venice, Italy, and the UK. She graduated in Management and Marketing at the University of Exeter where she penned the original version of this reflection, subsequently expanding it for inclusion in this book.

As a serial expatriate, Victoria has lived and worked in Europe, Central America, West Africa, Southeast Asia and the Middle East. Over the years, she has accumulated extensive experience in revenue acquisition, sales and marketing across diverse industries, such as stock photography, hospitality, and media.

In addition to her professional accomplishments, Victoria is also an award-winning photographer:

she was elected "Leader in Contemporary Art 2020" by Capsules Australia, recognised as one of the "100 Best Photographers 2021" by Photographize Magazine and is regularly featured in several artistic magazines and websites.

Victoria Schaal is reachable on LinkedIn and via email: vs@victoriaschaal.com

www.victoriaschaal.com

BY THE SAME AUTHOR:

THE BATTLEFIELD

I like to picture trade as a battlefield. Sellers are the infantry: foot soldiers who engage buyers one by one, commonly armed with persuasive speeches but often carrying heavier weapons like discounts. Marketing, on the other hand, is the artillery that lies back, atop the hill. It drops promotional bombs on large segments of audience in the hope of hitting as many buyers as possible or the powerful generals of big companies and organisations.

The study and making of marketing has proven to be extremely interesting to me since my teens: the relationship between marketing activities and the behaviour of society is a concept as complex as the human mind. People are different and as such, people behave differently. Different people like different things. Different people have different wants. Different people have different needs. Such a fact represents the labyrinthine trenches which sellers and marketers attempt to explore. This maze is the part of marketing that has always attracted me the most, both as an academic study and as a business tool.

However, due to my personal past experiences, which I will use in this reflection to draw examples, I found myself wondering whether there is room for altruism in such a battlefield. Can altruism exist and be part of my profession? We marketers are often heavily criticised and considered *bad guys*, paid off by villain big companies, who lie to get money out of naive consumers, who overcharge poor citizens, who create *fake needs* and so on.

Although I naturally nurture a drastically divergent vision of marketers, I do question us and our practices a great deal.

I thought that investigating the entire concept of altruism and apply my research and reflections to commercial marketing would contribute to clarify marketers' reasons and aims both in my head and in yours. I also thought that the investigation would reach deeper reflections and draw more reliable conclusions if I compared and contrasted the concepts of altruism and self-interest not solely in commercial marketing but especially in social marketing and in organisations that deem to fight egoism, such as NPOs.

HOW DO YOU LIKE IT?

www.ingramcontent.com/pod-product-compliance
Lightning Source LLC
Chambersburg PA
CBHW052256220526
45471CB00001B/357